RIDICULOUSLY SIMPLE SALES MANAGEMENT

RIDICULOUSLY SIMPLE SALES MANAGEMENT

How to Quickly Build and Maintain a
Successful, High-Performing Sales Team

STEVE STAUNING

Edited by Conner Stauning

ISBN: 9798683705381

Visit Steve Stauning on the web at www.SteveStauning.com
Also by Steve Stauning:

> *Assumptive Selling: The Complete Guide to Selling More Vehicles for More Money to Today's Connected Customers*
>
> *The 30,000-Pound Gorilla in the Room*
>
> *Sh*t Sandwich*

Contents

1. Successful Sales Management   1

2. The New Sales Manager   5

3. Sink or Swim   14

4. The Fallacy of Monthly Sales Goals   17

5. Lost in the Sauce   22

6. Attitude is (Almost) Everything   25

7. Be Dissatisfied   30

8. Motivation or Fauxtivation?   35

9. The Blame Game   39

10. The Trial Attorney   42

11. Sales Cures All Ills   46

12. Be Lazy   49

13. What You Don't Know   53

14. You are the Teacher   56

15. The Moneymakers   60

16. Driving Activities   64

17. Box Checking   72

18. Like or Respect?   77

19. Promos are not Panaceas   81

20. Be Satisfied   94

21. Creating Winners   96

22. The Legacy Sellers   105

23. Spinning the Plates   112

24. The "Secrets"   118

"The good news is that if salespeople always did what we wanted them to do, we never would've invented sales managers. The great news is this means you only need to train and reinforce best practices every single day for the rest of your working life."

Steve Stauning

"If the world were perfect, it wouldn't be."

Yogi Berra

This book was written for those personally leading sales teams and for every leader who has salespeople anywhere in their organizational chart. This includes owners, company presidents, vice presidents, general managers, and everyone else with "manager" in their title.

"Nothing happens until somebody sells something." This is a quote attributed to many successful leaders from Henry Ford to Peter Drucker; and it's a quote that should drive the priorities of your business.

But it doesn't matter if you're in sales or admin or you run the warehouse cleaning crew; if you're in management, your primary goal is the long-term health of your company. This means many things, but a healthy sales team should be near the top of your priorities – your admin or warehouse jobs just might depend on it.

After all, nothing happens until somebody sells something.

…

You may certainly read this book any way you choose. My recommendation would be to go slowly, taking in one chapter every three to seven days, and applying the lessons from that chapter immediately.

Each chapter is wrapped up with Key Learnings and Chapter Exercises. If you expect to get the most out of these – and want to see success with each chapter's exercises – tackling a chapter a week will likely work best for most sales managers.

1

SUCCESSFUL SALES MANAGEMENT

Before we dive into helping you and your sales team exceed your goals month after month, it's important to get two definitions out of the way. Throughout this book, I'm going to refer to *successful* sales managers and *unsuccessful* sales managers. And while not all managers who fall into one of these two categories are identical, there are some commonalities within each of these two broad classifications we should understand.

When referring to successful sales managers, I'm writing about those managers who routinely achieve real growth. Notice the word "real" in that sentence; it's important. Whether this growth is record sales, market share increases, profit growth, individual salesperson achievements, or all the above, the growth successful sales managers deliver is not due to some uncontrollable market swing.

That is, they're not just treading water in an up market, they are genuinely driving real growth. Oh, and the real growth they're driving is in both the short and long term. Successful sales managers aren't the whirlwinds who storm into an organization, generate great results for three to six months, and then disappear into the night as the sales team is left in shambles.

In a sentence, successful sales managers consistently drive real growth regardless of market conditions.

When I refer to unsuccessful sales managers, I'm referencing those managers who have little to do with their team's successes (and everything to do with their failures). Their sales are up a little when the market is up, and down a lot when the market is not. They struggle constantly with sales team turnover to the extent they'll always tell you they "just need to find some good people." They are great at making excuses and quick to point their fingers outward.

Unsuccessful sales managers are simply not maximizing the opportunities available. Instead, they accept what the market gives them.

Negative Coaching

There are multiple types of unsuccessful managers; and I'll mention some of their traits throughout this book. However, I'm not wasting a lot of ink detailing these because telling you what *not* to do is a form of negative coaching.

Negative coaching, interestingly, is one of the most common traits of unsuccessful sales managers; and I only mention it here to make you aware you might be caught up in this no-win waste of effort. Let me give you a quick example of a real-world coaching opportunity using both negative and positive coaching:

> SITUATION: You overheard a new salesperson asking a prospect how much they wanted to pay for a new car.
>
> NEGATIVE COACHING: "Are you crazy? Never ask them how much they want to pay! They'll always lowball you, and now you're having to negotiate up instead of forcing them to negotiate down!"
>
> POSITIVE COACHING: "When you asked that prospect how much they wanted to pay, what did they say?" … "And, how did that go?" … "What do you think you could do differently the next time to move your prospect closer to buying?"

Did you notice the positive coaching example was full of questions? We'll tackle why this works later; though for now, just contrast the two styles. Imagine if you were the new salesperson and ask yourself which style would help you grow your closing rates.

Negative coaching piles lots of "never do" and "stop doing" onto your psyche. It harms your self-esteem (which is pretty important in sales) and focuses you on what *not* to do. So much so, you constantly catch yourself doing the very things you've been telling yourself not to do. Yet, for some reason, you cannot seem to stop doing many of these.

Even delivered in a kind voice, constant negative coaching narrows a salesperson's imagination to what is possible. Instead of setting stretch goals and blowing these out of the water, salespeople subjected to constant negative coaching settle into mediocrity – that is, if they bother to remain in sales.

Certainly, all successful sales managers share some of what *not* to do with their sales teams. Often, they do so to shrink the learning curve. By sharing the mistakes they've made and what they've learned to sidestep, they can help new sellers avoid having to learn these lessons the hard way.

Of course, these negative coaching lessons are immediately followed by the successful sales manager modeling best practices. When you do this, you move the salesperson's focus from the negative (stop doing) to the positive (start doing).

What to Expect

"Okay," you say, "I'm all-in on this whole successful sales management thingy; but I want to know what to expect." More specifically, "What will the lessons in this book bring me, my team, and our organization?"

Great question… and I'm glad you asked that.

Of course, we already know that successful sales managers drive sustained, real growth. That's certainly a great reason to embrace these lessons. However, there are even greater benefits to becoming a successful sales manager for you, your team, and your organization. Some of these are so below the surface that you wouldn't normally recognize them as benefits if I didn't list them here.

For example, successful sales managers know why their teams are successful. Unsuccessful sales managers do not. The great benefit here is that if results flatten (and they will from time to time), you know instantly how to make course corrections that quickly get your team back on track.

Contrast this with a sales manager just taking what the market gives. If the market flattens (or worse), how will that manager be able to grow sales? They had no idea why their sales were up in the past and have no idea why they're down now.

Other hidden benefits? I'll briefly list a few here and explore these more in the coming lessons:

> Successful sales managers are happier and have less bad stress than unsuccessful sales managers. (We'll discuss the two primary types of stress – distress and eustress – in the "Spinning the Plates" chapter.)
>
> Successful sales managers control their own success.
>
> Successful sales managers enjoy nearly zero negative turnover.
>
> Successful sales managers offload the unimportant. (The vendor calls, the admin garbage, the busy work, etc.)

Imagine that! Successful sales managers are happier, in control, and aren't burdened by the never-ending search for new salespeople or busy work. Sounds like a meaningful goal to pursue!

The Good News and Great News

Let's close this chapter with how we opened this book; the good news and the great news about sales management.

The good news is that if salespeople always did what we wanted them to do, we never would've invented sales managers.

The great news is this means you only need to train and reinforce best practices every single day for the rest of your working life.

...

KEY LEARNINGS:

- Successful sales managers control their success.

- Because of this, successful sales managers know why their results are up, and they know what to do when they're not.

- The job of sales management is never done; but, successful sales managers are happier and more productive doing the job.

CHAPTER EXERCISES:

- Consider your last few interactions with your sales team until you find one example where you provided negative coaching. That is, where you explained what *not* to do, instead of what to do.

- Replay this interaction in your mind (and perhaps in writing) and change your coaching response to one that (a) asks more questions, and (b) models the behavior you're looking to instill in your team.

- How will you change your future approach to similar opportunities?

2

THE NEW SALES MANAGER

While this chapter was written for those starting with a new team, feel free to use these lessons if your team needs a reset. In fact, if you're reading this book, there's a good chance your team needs a reset.

Rare is the manager who starts a team from scratch. Most often, someone is promoted from within a team or promoted/hired from outside the group to take over an existing team.

When someone on a sales team is promoted from a salesperson role to that of a sales manager, for example, they already know and understand the team dynamics, the personalities, the customers, the challenges, and the company goals. Provided they have the necessary intelligence, business acumen, and leadership skills to be successful, they should be able to hit the ground running and never look back.

However, how does a new manager – that is, one hired from outside the group or organization – set the stage for success without spending months getting up to speed?

In this chapter, I'll share with you some tips and tactics I used when I was hired to take over an outside B2B sales team that was ranked last in their region. In six short months, this team became the number one sales team in volume and volume growth, and they held that position for the next 50 consecutive months.

Much of that success is due in large part to the stage that was set in the first two days.

It's All in the Preparation

Officially hired 21 days before I was set to take over, I asked the general manager for the following documents before I met the team:

- Salespeople names, dates of hire, YTD compensation, and territories;

- The previous five years of company sales and distribution figures;

- A SWOT analysis of the top three competitors;

- Current year sales goals for all product lines and YTD results; and

- The GM's expectations for the position.

I also spent about ten days in this company's market, visiting with their customers, while mystery shopping and (secretly) observing the sales team.

After reviewing the documents and spending time in the market, it was clear to me that this team lacked execution and direction (of course, you could surmise this given their last-place ranking). Everyone appeared to be working very hard, but they were failing miserably at actually doing things that mattered. Additionally, I discovered that this group's prior leader had been very hands-on with the largest customers – so much so that he was figuratively cutting the legs out from under his team.

I felt like this group needed to see real change – not just a new butt behind the sales manager's desk – so I got permission from the GM to access the salesroom and rearrange a few things the weekend before I started.

Day One for the New Sales Manager

As the sales team staggered in between 8:30 and 9:00 AM on Monday, they were quite shocked to see that their salesroom bore no resemblance to the one they left on Friday.

While I understand that most people don't like sudden change, and no one really likes surprise changes made to their personal spaces, this group was in last place and needed this proverbial "slap in the face." So, I slapped them as hard as I could without actually hurting anyone.

Where they once had blank walls, they now had displays of every one of their company's products (complete with point-of-sale merchandise). On the formerly clean windows, they now saw up-to-date charts, graphs, and spreadsheets detailing every key performance metric for their team and the other teams in the region. They also saw weighted salesperson rankings that showed definitively who was performing and who was not.

The most striking change, however, was in the form of their seating arrangements. Where this "team" once had twenty small cubicles, they now had one very large table and a wall of short file cabinets labeled with their names. No longer would this group act as individuals – this new arrangement would prove to guarantee both best practices sharing and shorter office stays. (Unless an outside salesperson sells with a telephone, there is no reason for them to be in the office except for training and, in the old days before direct deposit, to pick up a paycheck.)

The grumbling was comically animated. I still chuckle today when I picture the mix of blank stares and angry glances – these reactions made giving up my entire weekend worthwhile.

I emerged from my new office and greeted the team as they arrived. I introduced myself to every one of them the same way: "Hi, I'm the new sales manager, and my only job is to support you."

The First Sales Meeting

Like most sales teams, this group held long rah-rah sessions once a week to "fire up the troops." From what the GM told me, these were often very inspirational, though they never seemed to translate into solid results. Everyone would leave the meeting with great enthusiasm only to come back to the office on Friday reporting subpar sales.

This told me the team lacked an understanding of their goals, clear direction, and the support necessary to execute those goals. I decided that my first meeting must not be about motivation, but expectations – both my expectations of them and, more importantly, what they could expect from me. Here is a synopsis of what I showed and told them when I stood in front of them for the first time:

What you can expect from me…

- I will always be fair, open, and honest.

- I will check my ego at the door.

- I will always respect you by being on time to our appointments and meetings.

- I will keep my meetings short and informative.

- I believe that those closest to the customers should make the decisions – you are closest to the customer.

- I will never shoot you for making a bad decision provided you made it with the best intentions.

- I believe that "the way we always did it" is not working and we need to find a new way to do things.

- My primary goal is to help you make this company number one in the country – we are currently last in our region.

- You are the only ones who can guarantee we are successful in that goal.

- This will never be about me; it will always be about you – you are the only people in this company who create revenue.

- If you are not in sales, then you are in support – I am in support and my only job is to make you the hero.

- I will always keep my word and I will always honor your commitments to the customers, even when it costs the company money.

What I expect from you…

- I expect you to always be fair, open, and honest.

- I expect you to have a healthy ego.

- I expect you to be on time to meetings – if you're late for our sales meetings, how can I believe you'll be on time for customer appointments?

- I expect you to contribute to meetings by having a success story to share each week.

- I expect you to make decisions for yourself.

- I expect you to fail tremendously. This will ensure that you have tremendous successes. Besides, if you're not failing, then I know you're not trying.

- I expect you to learn from your failures.

- I never want to hear why we can't do something; I only want to hear ways we can. In other words, stop placing roadblocks in the way of your success.

- I expect you to be the number one salesperson in the company – yes, I expect each and every one of you to be number one.

- I expect you to be the hero and to never let anyone in this company, especially me, cut your legs out from under you.

- I expect you to always keep your word to your customers, even when it costs the company money.

- I expect you to stand on my desk and scream at me if I ever fail to live up to your expectations.

A lot to digest, I know. However, without setting clear expectations for both sides on the very first day, new sales managers will miss the greatest opportunity to gain the attention of their team. Each day that goes by without delivering clear direction and expectations makes it harder to drive real success from an existing team.

Of course, the same applies to hiring new salespeople. Successful sales managers set the expectations on Day One (or even during the interview). They don't wait for new salespeople to develop bad habits.

Their Reaction?

Prior to my arrival, this group was always told what to do and when to do it. The previous sales manager was the superstar and the salespeople were his roadies. It was always about him and never about them.

Given this, they were putty in my hands after that speech. Good salespeople need direction, while great sellers thrive on it.

Of course, this presentation was just words unless I was prepared to live it, and live it I did. From cosmetic changes like removing the reserved parking sign for the sales manager to real changes like showing up unannounced to help a salesperson working on a Saturday, I lived the vision I described, and the reps took notice.

The New Manager Questionnaire

At the end of this first meeting, I distributed a questionnaire (posted below) and arranged a time to meet with each rep for one-on-one sessions to discuss their answers. Although we had 20 salespeople at the time, I really wanted to get these all done quickly, so I opened my schedule from 6:30 a.m. to 9:00 p.m. the following day and allowed the salespeople to select their own meeting times.

The questionnaire was designed to give me a sense of who they were, provide them an avenue to vent about whatever it was that needed changing, and to deliver a measure of self-awareness to this underperforming group.

In many ways, this questionnaire contains the best questions you can ask your new sales team. It quickly provides you much of the information you need to lead, while bringing to the surface any current or potential issues that could derail the team's future sales success.

Salesperson Questionnaire:

1. Where do you see yourself in 1 year? 3 years? 10 years?

2. What three things do you like most about your job?

3. What three things do you like least about your job?

4. If you could change anything about our company, what would it be and how would you change it?

5. What should we absolutely start doing today that we're currently not doing?

6. What should we absolutely stop doing today that we're currently doing?

7. What should we absolutely continue doing that we're currently doing?

8. How would you describe our company to a close friend?

9. Describe the quality and quantity of training you feel you've received since coming to work here. What gaps exist in the training we've provided?

10. Describe your abilities as they relate to your current position.

11. Is there a different position within our company you feel better suited for other than salesperson? If so, what is that position and why do you feel that way?

12. What is your total compensation? (Include your base, bonus, and any perks like car allowances.)

13. What should be your total compensation and how can I help you achieve this?

14. Were there ever any promises made to you by anyone at our company that have not been kept? If so, please detail these.

15. How many hours per week do you estimate you dedicate to achieving your goals at this company?

16. In order to become the number one salesperson in the region, how many hours a week do you think you would need to commit to the company?

17. What must be done to grow revenue and profit in your territory?

18. What must be done to grow revenue and profit for the whole company?

19. On a scale of 1-10, rate the selling ability of each of the other salespeople and yourself.

20. How would you prefer to be managed?

Why These 20 Questions?

Why are these likely the 20 best questions to ask your new sales team? With these 20 questions, you'll learn more about your marketplace and your reps' ability to execute than you will with months of observations. Each question was designed to elicit a specific response or trigger a specific paradigm shift in the salesperson:

- Questions 1 and 11 tell you if they have ambitions beyond being a salesperson, and how to plan a career path for each sales rep.

- Questions 2, 3, and 20 tell you how to manage the respective rep. (I put Question 20 last because this one usually provides some great dialogue and an easy transition for a handshake and an, "I'll do my best, please keep me in line" from me.)

- Question 4 tells you if this person is just a complainer or someone who's given real thought to the issues at hand and believes they know how to fix them.

- Questions 5 through 8 tell you how to manage up and across. (That is, what you need to gain for your team from the other department heads and from your supervisor.)

- Questions 9 and 10 set the stage for the amount and type of sales training and product training that needs to occur quickly.

- Questions 12 and 13 help you understand how much motivation money provides to a particular salesperson.

- Question 14 helps you remove all the animosity of previously broken promises (and every sales team is full of broken promises from the company). Of course, this is true only if you honor the broken promises of your predecessor. (Or explain in detail why you cannot.)

- Questions 15, 16, and 17 are really kind of cool, because they reveal to the salesperson, out loud, that they're probably not giving all they can.

- The aggregated answers to Question 18 will help you create plans to reach the company's goals. (The salespeople really do have all the answers, you just need to ask them.)

- Question 19 gives you a sense of how everyone views their teammates, and which ones are the leaders and which ones may need development, retraining, or a new career.

I asked the sales team to come prepared to answer all these questions during their one-on-one meetings, but that they didn't need to bring anything written – I would take copious notes (which I did).

Hearing a sales rep tell you, out loud, that he's a 5 on a 1-10 scale is extremely powerful. This is someone eager to learn; and the self-realization that occurs by voicing their score out loud gives them a voracious appetite for direction, development, and sales training.

Do You Really Mean It?

Good salespeople are good because they can read people, and they'll always know when you're lying. The key to this questionnaire is sincerity. You must be sincere about wanting to know the answers to these questions, and you must be sincere about wanting to change the things that need changing. If all you do is ask the questions and take no action, your team will never trust you and they will never outperform.

…

The lessons included throughout the rest of this book will give you what you need to use your team's answers to create and maintain the best sales team in your district, region, whatever. Suffice it to say that sharing a vision (what I said in my first meeting) and then living that vision can do wonders for a rag-tag group like the one I inherited.

…

KEY LEARNINGS:

- Make your first impression count. Taking your time to "get up to speed" before sharing your vision and creating two-way expectations generally ensures failure.

- Don't be afraid to take charge immediately. Just as I rearranged the salesroom before my first day, make your presence known early and leave little doubt about your intentions. (Certainly, if you're taking over a high-performing team, you're not going to turn their world upside down on Day One, but there should be no doubt about your role.)

- If you're not selling, then you're support. As a sales manager, your only job is to support your sales team. Live this and the other expectations I laid out for myself.

CHAPTER EXERCISES:

- Create a list of those things your team should expect from you.

- Based on this list, would you want to work for you?

- If yes, then share these with your team (even if you've been their manager for a decade).

- If no, then create a new list.

- If you plan to make large cultural, structural, or process changes based on what you read in this book, consider a reset meeting with your sales team that you treat like the first day sales meeting I described.

3

SINK OR SWIM

While training and consulting with a client – working with the sales team at a struggling automotive retailer – I was pulled aside by one of the sales managers who told me not to bother with salespeople X, Y, and Z because, in his words, "I don't think they're going to make it."

Yikes. What year is this? Not going to make it? Why not? Why did you hire them in the first place? Who did you assign to mentor them? What makes you think your next three new hires are going to fare any better than X, Y, and Z?

To make this revelation even more startling, the sales manager who told me this was the same one who hired these three after an extensive interview process. All three had been on the job less than 90 days; and all three were replacing other newbies who also (coincidentally) didn't "make it."

During the time of this consultation, the economy was chugging along, and the unemployment rate was at an historic low. This meant the candidate pool was shallow; and the manager shouldn't expect the next batch of three new sellers would perform any better.

However, regardless of the state of the job market, it's time to come to grips with something in sales. That is, we're way beyond the old school sink or swim.

Sink or Swim

For decades, sales managers were semi-successful hiring a bunch of newbies and throwing them in the river of sales. Those few that didn't drown were deemed to be good salespeople; while those that sank "just weren't cut out for sales."

Companies could operate this way because there was an almost endless supply of fresh meat – and there was no internet where the underemployed, dissatisfied, or overqualified could easily find a better gig. (And, no internet where potential new hires could learn how crappy it is to work for a given management team.)

Times have changed. Young people aren't that interested in sales positions. The hours, the training, the talking to people face-to-face or over the phone scares the crap out of most millennials and Gen Z's. Throwing wave after wave of new hires into the river to see who swims doesn't create great sales teams; it just creates revenue for staffing agencies and job security for your HR department.

Plus, as has always been the case, new hires with the skill sets to become great salespeople won't reach anywhere near their potential without great leadership. They'll drown. Moreover, hiring great veteran sellers isn't the answer because great salespeople won't work for bad leaders.

Let's be clear, selling isn't hard... it just takes work.

Likewise, creating great sellers isn't hard... it just takes work.

Helping Everyone Swim

Because we no longer have the luxury of sink or swim, sales managers who want to escape the endless cycle of recruiting, hiring, firing, recruiting, hiring, firing, etc. can work to create a simple mentoring program within their team. It's not hard to do; and it certainly requires no outside help (hint: your top sellers or assistant managers can and should do this).

The solution is simple and effective: Assign a manager, assistant manager, or senior salesperson to every new hire. It's now this manager's or salesperson's job to make sure X or Y or Z is successful. Offer a bonus when X reaches a predetermined sales objective. Also, give them a bonus when their trainee reaches certain employment milestones (like 6 months, 12 months, etc.). Finally, make sure the assigned manager or salesperson knows that if X doesn't make it, they'll be assigned X2... and then X3... and then X4.

Oh crap, that sounds like someone will be accountable for the new hire's success; that they'll be responsible for ensuring the business does everything it can to help their new hire swim.

Oh. The. Humanity.

It's amazing what accountability and responsibility can accomplish.

Ten Burger King Fry Cooks

While it's not true in every industry, I've often said of car dealers that you could hire ten Burger King fry cooks and put them under a great sales manager. Fast forward six months, and that sales manager would have eight or nine high-performing sellers.

Conversely, you could hire ten superstar sellers and put them under a lousy sales manager. Fast forward six months, and that sales manager would have three mediocre salespeople remaining from the original ten superstars. Plus, the lousy sales manager would be lamenting the need to find some good people.

The point of this hypothetical example is simple: It's not who you hire, it's how you lead. Great sales managers will find ways for their teams to succeed, while lousy sales managers will suck the life out of even the best salespeople. Those working for the former will reach their full potential. Those working for the latter will either quit or settle into the mediocrity that's accepted in low-performing sales organizations.

…

KEY LEARNINGS:

- It's not who you hire, it's how you lead.

- Make the most with what you've got. There's no guarantee the next new hires are going to be any better than the ones you've got now.

- Without accountability to a new hire's success, there's no incentive to ensure they succeed – and no disincentive if they do not.

CHAPTER EXERCISES:

- Rethink your your entire onboarding process; and build it in a way that maximizes the chances for success for new sellers.

- Assign someone to mentor each new salesperson and those who are performing below expectations.

- Give the mentor some stake in the success or failure of those they are assigned to mentor.

4

THE FALLACY OF MONTHLY SALES GOALS

See if this sounds familiar.

It's the first day of the new month and the sales manager is standing in the front of the room holding a marker. On the board behind him or her are the names of all the salespeople with their final sales tallies from last month.

The sales manager goes around the room asking each seller what their goal is for this month.

> MANAGER: "Bob, how many you gonna do this month?"
>
> BOB: "25!"
>
> MANAGER: "Excellent! Twenty-five it is!"

The manager writes "25" next to Bob's name, and this activity continues until every seller has "committed" to a goal for this month.

Except, there was no commitment. No plan. Even worse, there will be no accountability to these alleged goals. On the first day of the next month, Bob's 25 will be erased, and his actual results posted, so the monthly exercise in futility can be repeated.

The Fallacy of Monthly Sales Goals

I'm hopeful you see the fallacy here… strike that. I'm hopeful you see the insanity here. Writing a number on the board does not make it so. Moreover, expecting your salespeople to focus on their artificial goal – to work as hard as they can to achieve this goal – is lunacy. Most people aren't built that way.

Most people – and this includes most salespeople – are *not* self-motivated to succeed. They want success, but they are self-motivated to take the easy way when given a choice. For example, if the choice is to make prospecting calls or play a game on their iPhone, they'll choose the latter. Even though they know making prospecting calls will make them more money.

Allowing salespeople to set their own goals is a great strategy... if you plan to follow through and help them achieve these goals. It's a great strategy because if they set a goal that's too low, you can challenge them immediately with a friendly, public ribbing.

> MANAGER: "Twenty-five? Come 'on Bob, you're better than that."

Of course, when they set a true stretch goal, you can challenge them immediately to let you and the rest of the team know how they're going to accomplish this.

> MANAGER: "Excellent! Twenty-five it is! Now, tell me how we're going to get there?"

That last word track is a hallmark of something I call a Show Me Leader. A leader who asks lots of great questions, and then follows up their subordinate's response with something like, "Great, show me."

As I'll explain a few times this book, being a Show Me Leader is the easiest and least-combative way to push a sales team to achieve great success. It allows you to challenge your team, hold them accountable, and drive sales activities with simple questions that are taken as helpful, rather than accusatory.

Back to Bob's 25

For many valid reasons (too many other duties, too many subordinates, wrong pay plan, etc.) and some invalid reasons (lazy, apathetic, schadenfreude – look it up or read about it in a later chapter), sales managers often struggle to properly motivate their charges to reach stretch goals.

Of course, this should be their primary duty. That is, ensuring their salespeople maximize their true sales potential. Let's look at how Bob's earlier goal of 25 plays out in the real world. In this example, Bob sells cars for a busy dealership.

- Bob sets an artificial goal of 25 for this month after selling 20 last month.

- Bob is then left alone to sink or swim for the next 30 days.

- On the 15th of the month, Bob has 14 units sold.

- When the month ends, Bob finishes with 19-21 units.

- All this, despite the fact he was pacing 28+ at mid-month.

Underachieving on artificial goals represents a typical month for the typical car salesperson in America. Of course, that's okay because no one is going to hold Bob accountable to the 25 he said he was going to sell anyway.

Sell One Today

Interestingly, with just one small change in the sales manager's leadership approach, Bob would've sold 30+. The one small change? Asking, "How can I help you sell one today?" and then, of course, acting on this.

The concept of "sell one today" is not new. It's how most automotive salespeople selling 30+ approach each day. They challenge themselves to sell one today – which is a daily goal; and daily goals are more effective at driving success than monthly goals.

For the 20-car (or worse) folks on your team, it's up to you, the sales manager, to instill this in their daily routine. It's also – and this is the most important part of driving sales success – squarely on your shoulders to help everyone on your team sell one today. (The concept of "sell one today" can be applied to any industry, of course.)

This begins as soon as the salespeople arrive to start their shift. Don't let them mill about for an hour; don't wait for them to get in their groove; don't let them join the vaping circle; don't even let them get their coffee!

"But Steve, I have a lot on my plate when I get to work. It's impossible for me to meet with the team until about 10 or 11!"

Get there early. If you can't get there early, then pause your admin duties for about ten minutes while you hold a quick meeting with all salespeople – yes, even the 30-car guys and gals. You only need to say one thing, and mean it, at this meeting:

> "Everyone needs to sell one today – whatever it takes. After you've sold one, then your goal is to sell one more. After that, one more. The great news is that as soon as I finish (the morning paperwork/ordering cars/whatever), I'm going to help each of you sell one today. Now, go find that one sale you're going to make today and invite them in for an appointment."

Now What?

Now we do a little something that's been successful for about 50 years: MBWA – management by walking around. This means, when you're done with whatever administrative duties you're saddled with every morning, you get up and walk around.

You take a couple of minutes with each of your sellers – at their workstations – and you become a Show Me Leader:

> MANAGER: "Do you have at least one sale planned for today?"
>
> BOB: (It doesn't matter how Bob replies.)
>
> MANAGER: "Great! Show me."

While not obvious at first, eventually your salespeople will know what "show me" means. If they just told you they can't find any good prospects, they'll show what they've been doing, and you'll help them find someone to sell by pointing them in a new direction (database, internet lead, unsold follow-up, service drive, etc.).

If they just told you they've got an appointment scheduled for today, they'll proudly show this prospect. Congratulate them and then challenge them to set two more appointments. Also, tell this salesperson you'll help them find these two additional prospects if they cannot do so on their own.

Attitude and Activity

Congratulations! You're now executing on the two most important factors that lead to sales success: Attitude and Activity. Your attitude: that every salesperson can and should sell one today, is driving their activities. Additionally, you've instilled in them an expectation that they must sell one today. (We'll explore more about attitude and activities throughout this book.)

The idea that I will sell one today is a powerful driver of success, and a much better goal than the one Bob set for himself at the beginning of the month.

The result? Most of your team will sell one or more units today… and tomorrow… and the next day… and the next. Your 20-car seller with the 25-car goal will look up at the board on the last day of the month and see 33!

Their confidence and their attitude will improve alongside their paycheck. Their life will never be the same again – that is, as long as you continue to help them sell one today, of course.

…

KEY LEARNINGS:

- Being a Show Me Leader is the easiest way to drive sales success.

- Daily goals are better and more effective than monthly goals.

- Left alone, most salespeople will gravitate toward the easy.

CHAPTER EXERCISES:

- Practice being a Show Me Leader today. Find a situation where the use of questions followed by "show me" will help you uncover roadblocks and/or drive the sales activities that lead to success.

- Keep your monthly goals; however, break these down by day, and start each day reviewing that day's goals and month-to-date results with individual sellers.

5

LOST IN THE SAUCE

Most sales managers wear many hats. They're not just their team's sales leader, they're also responsible for other productive and (unfortunately) unproductive tasks. As a sales manager with duties that go beyond merely supervising your team, it's easy to get lost in the sauce.

"Lost in the sauce" is a slang term most often used to describe someone who is intoxicated or who is happily confused. For our purposes, sales managers who get lost in the sauce are those so focused on the trivial they forget the important.

Just as we learned in the last chapter that most salespeople will gravitate toward the easy, the same is true for most sales managers. The difference for sales managers is they're not playing games on their smartphones; they're caught up in the hamster wheel of never-ending busywork.

Busy vs Productive

Let's start by formalizing your overriding goal – some call this the "big G Goal," where the G is capitalized to indicate it's the most important goal.

If you're reading this book, then your overriding goal is probably to maximize sales and profit in the short and long term. Whatever your big G Goal, write it down and post it somewhere you'll constantly see it. Now, let's learn the most important and basic decision-making formula you'll ever use:

> Things that take me closer to my goal are good; things that take me away from my goal are bad.

While not every situation or opportunity where a decision is required will be easily answered by this formula, most will. In fact, you'll likely be surprised how often this simple sentence helps you make better decisions more quickly.

Especially with how you use your time.

Most unsuccessful sales managers get caught up in reports, administrative work, and similar minutia. They believe they are productive because they were busy all day; their day was hectic and filled with activities. Unfortunately, their activity didn't equal sales success for their team today. They were lost in the sauce… perhaps they'll have better luck tomorrow.

Productive activities take you closer to your goal; busywork takes you farther away.

Leading is Leading

Completing reports is not leading.

Analyzing data is not leading.

Meeting with vendors or other departments is not leading.

Only leading is leading.

While some of those reports you compiled, some of the data you analyzed, and some of the meetings you attended will lead you closer to your goal, the sad reality is most will not. In fact, most will take you farther from your goal.

Avoid at all Costs

Telling you to avoid something is a form of negative coaching; and I wish there was a positive coaching way to say this, but there's not.

Avoid getting lost in the sauce at all costs.

Start by reviewing your days in real time. For some of you, this means keeping a pad of paper on your desk where you track the time you start and end each activity. For others, it might mean listing what you do throughout the day without times attached. Either plan is effective to help you become a more effective sales leader.

Briefly review yesterday's list each morning and simply put a plus (+) or minus sign (-) next to each activity. The pluses indicate activities that took you closer to your goal; the minuses, of course, represent the opposite. Where you're unsure about an activity, put a minus sign. Anything that takes your time and attention but does not bring you closer to your goal is taking you away from an activity that could bring you closer.

Are you shocked by how many meaningless activities you find yourself immersed in each day?

Congratulations, you've unlocked an important secret to sales success that some call time management. I, on the other hand, call it self-awareness. Now that you're aware of all the unimportant duties and responsibilities you or others have thrust upon you, you can begin to dig yourself out of the minutia and free up your day to start leading.

Manage Up

While I understand there are probably bureaucracies within your organization that find these activities important, it's incumbent upon you to manage up. That is, take your list of minuses to the powers that be and explain in plain, though respectful language that these tasks are unimportant, and they are hurting your team's ability to maximize sales results.

The two possible outcomes of this exercise are both okay. One, your boss tells you why these activities are important, allowing you to put the proper focus on them moving forward. Or two, your boss agrees with you and the activities are cast aside, freeing up your day.

…

KEY LEARNINGS:

- Busy does not mean productive.

- Things that take you closer to your goal are good; things that take you away from your goal are bad.

CHAPTER EXERCISES:

- The exercise from this chapter is spelled out for you. Start today: Write down your big G Goal and begin tracking how you really spend your time.

6

ATTITUDE IS (ALMOST) EVERYTHING

Way back in the 1980s, tennis great Andre Agassi famously said, "Image is everything." Of course, he was pitching Canon cameras, and the line was written for him. But… I digress.

For sustained sales success, it's attitude, not image. And for sales managers wanting to drive better results, attitude is almost everything.

For more than a decade, I've been training sales teams for car dealers, dealer groups, manufacturers, and vendors. Over that time, the difference between success and failure for these sales teams has always come down to just two things: attitude and activity. I've called these the two "secrets" to driving growth – with "secrets" in quotes – because they're not really secrets at all.

The Two "Secrets" to Driving Growth

The primary issues impacting your business (turnover, flat sales, declining profits, missed opportunities) are not the result of not knowing what to do. Your sales team already knows what to do… they're just not doing it.

In some cases, they're infected with the wrong attitude and focused on unimportant activities. In most cases, managers are simply not aware how attitude impacts the bottom line, while their salespeople have no focus on any activities, important or unimportant.

As a sales manager, understanding the importance of your involvement in cultivating the proper attitude and driving the right activities is critical to creating a team of high performers.

Secret #1: Attitude

Regardless of the economy or the current unemployment rate, we've already discussed that the time has long passed when your company could afford to hire a bunch of new salespeople and just throw them in the river of sales. We're way beyond sink or swim with new hires.

Millennials and Gen Z's won't work for jerks. They don't need to; there are too many other opportunities out there. Moreover, unlike the sales game of 20 years ago, great salespeople aren't willing to eat crap served by a directionless prick with a bad attitude. Salespeople young and old realize that life's too short to work for jerks.

Your attitude affects their attitudes. In fact, your attitude affects everything. Let's compare the attitudes of my best clients with those of the average underperforming sales team.

Love What You Do

Managers on high-performing teams truly love what they do; and they feel blessed being in their current role. Conversely, no one seems happy with their vocational choice when I visit underperforming companies.

Of course, you're probably thinking that managers at top companies love what they do because they get to work for a top company. Not even close; in fact, it's the exact opposite. Their companies outperform precisely because these managers come prepared with a great attitude every day.

The positive attitude of the owner/president drives the positive attitudes of his or her managers.

The positive attitudes of the managers drive the positive attitudes of their salespeople.

Moreover, those at the top of your organization choose to be positive or negative – the rest of the team then becomes "infected" by whatever choice you and your managers make. Both positivity and negativity have the capability to shape the hearts and minds of your team. And, as you probably know, you can "buy" a salesperson's back, but you must win his or her heart and mind.

Regardless of where you work or what you do, loving what you do is a choice. Your choice. Choose wisely.

Everyone's a Buyer

Truer today than ever before: everyone is a buyer. They really are. For those teams selling to the general public, by the time the average consumer sends in a lead, picks up a phone, or walks in your store, they are ready to buy… they just need someone to help them buy today.

There is a pervasive attitude in the B2C companies growing market share. That is, to a person, they will do what it takes to make the deal. This doesn't mean their profits suffer – to the contrary; they also happen to make more profit per sale than underperforming teams.

It simply means that from top to bottom, the entire team agrees that everyone's a buyer who wants to buy today. More importantly, they approach every opportunity with this belief.

Once your salespeople believe everyone's a buyer who wants to buy today, the faster they'll respond to leads, the better they'll handle their phone calls, and the quicker they'll pull customers through your road-to-the-sale. They'll also approach these tasks with more confidence.

However, if this attitude is not driven from the top, your managers will kill more deals than they save.

When sales managers in automotive retail believe everyone's a buyer who wants to buy today, they'll greet every guest before the test drive (called Early Manager Introduction, and it's proven to speed up the sale and close more deals at higher gross profits); they'll ensure 100% of the guests are properly logged in the CRM; and they'll conduct proactive customer interventions (called TO's or turnovers in automotive) because they know when a customer has been on the lot for two hours without being presented a deal.

Why wouldn't they do all this? I mean, if you were certain someone was buying today… someplace… wouldn't you do everything you could to ensure they bought from you?

Of course, the minute you or your salespeople believe someone is not a buyer, you'll be 100% right.

Their Success is Your Success

As crazy as it sounds, I still run into managers who resent the success of their top sellers. You read that right: businesses are full of old-school managers who either because of envy or fear (or both), begrudge the accomplishments (and the paychecks) of their best people.

Not surprisingly, these top sellers often leave… or worse: settle into the mediocrity that is celebrated by their underperforming managers.

Sales managers who understand and truly believe that the success of their team is their success are almost there when it comes to attitude. Their next step is simply to redirect their encounters with these teams from "chastising and mandating" to "coaching and mentoring."

Think about it. If 90% of your subordinate interactions consist of you bashing them, why in the world would they want to outperform for you? This includes owners/executives speaking to their general managers, general managers speaking to their sales managers, and sales managers speaking to their salespeople.

If you truly believe that your team's success is your success, you'd never chastise; you'd always coach.

The Attitude Checklist

Consistent across all my top performing clients is a simple, unwritten attitude checklist in the minds of every manager:

- I love what I do, and I'm blessed to be here today.

- Everyone is a buyer who wants to buy today.

- I want every person on my team to succeed.

Conversely, most sales managers at underperforming companies believe just the opposite.

Of course, attitude is only half the equation. I've worked with company owners and managers who have terrific attitudes, yet their company is still just treading water. Why? Simple; they're afraid to drive the activities that deliver results.

Basically, they're a bunch of really nice guys and gals who allow mediocrity because they're missing the second "secret" to driving growth. We'll hit that "secret" later in the book. For now, let's keep your focus on attitude.

…

KEY LEARNINGS:

- Your attitude affects and infects the attitude of your team.

- Believing everyone is a buyer creates confidence; believing the opposite ensures failure.

CHAPTER EXERCISES:

- Take an honest look at both your internal and external attitudes. Do these align with the attitude checklist?

- If you don't love what you do, find a way to start loving it or find a new gig.

- If you don't genuinely want everyone on your team to succeed, it's time to uncover the problem. (Hint: You'll locate the problem with a quick glance in a mirror.)

7

BE DISSATISFIED

Plainly stated, successful sales managers are dissatisfied. Successful salespeople are dissatisfied.

Of course, this doesn't mean they're unhappy. To the contrary, top sales managers and top sellers are extremely happy; however, they understand good is the enemy of great. Last month was good; this month will be great.

"But Steve, what if last month wasn't just good; what if it was a record month?" You ask.

I'm glad you asked that.

After a record month, great salespeople and great sales managers don't relax and admire what they sold. Instead, they look at where they can improve as they begin planning and working to beat that record this month. They are dissatisfied... if you will.

Continuous Improvement Requires Dissatisfaction

Success in sales is not one sale – regardless of how hard you worked to achieve it. It's also not one day, one week, one month, or even one year. Success in sales is a never-ending quest to continuously increase and maximize all available opportunities. It's a goal, for lack of a better term, that you never actually achieve.

We can and should celebrate our wins. Successful sales managers do just that. They do this to reward and motivate their teams to do even more. But, when this celebration leads to contentment, sellers (and sales teams) will always return to their pre-record averages.

If you're a sales manager in automotive retail, let's see if this scenario sounds familiar:

> One of your salespeople, Janelle, has been averaging around fifteen units a month for the last year. Last month, you worked with Janelle a little

more than usual; she had some deals go her way that she would've lost in the past; and she ended the month with a solid 23 units sold at good grosses. A personal best for Janelle.

This represents a 53% increase over her average units and a 53% (or more) increase in her paycheck!

Janelle was thrilled! You were thrilled!

Fast forward to the end of this month, and she sold thirteen.

What happened? You showed her how to sell more. You helped her sell more. Janelle, like most of your sellers, is motivated by money. She sets goals every month… yet, she went backward.

Regression to the Mean

Janelle, it turns out, was just lucky when she sold 23.

"Bull!" You exclaim, "I worked with her; she worked hard; she had a great attitude the whole month!"

That's all true, of course; though, it's missing one point. Math doesn't lie.

Janelle regressed to the mean (average). She's an average fifteen-car seller. This means, over time, she's going to average fifteen. Twenty-three was a fluke.

I already wrote she had some deals go her way that she would've lost in the past. Maybe she faced easier buyers that month; perhaps her prospects had better overall credit scores; possibly her managers took a few "skinny" deals they would've passed on in prior months. All we know is that she regressed to the mean.

The best way to explain regression to the mean is to use the example many others have used: The *Sports Illustrated* Jinx.

The "jinx" basically goes like this: When an athlete appears on the cover of *Sports Illustrated*, their subsequent performance is going to decline. Of course, any sane person who understands math knows there's no such thing as a jinx; the decline in their stats is simply regression to the mean.

The athlete made the cover of *Sports Illustrated* because of an outstanding performance. Perhaps a great game, week, month, or year. But that performance was most often just a lucky streak. Over time, this athlete performs at their average. Some weeks/months above their average and some below.

Because their outstanding performance landed them on the cover – and their subsequent performances bring them back to average – the blame was placed on the jinx.

Baseball provides the best example of this because MLB teams play 162 regular season games in a normal year. The average MLB batter hits .250. However, if we broke out an average hitter's performance on a weekly basis, you'd find weeks where he batted .125 and weeks where he batted .375. Was he a better batsman in the .375 weeks than in the .125 weeks? If so, why can't he always bat .375?

Because he was lucky during the .375 weeks and unlucky in the .125 weeks. He got more balls to break his way in the good weeks; more bloop singles; more pitchers who "didn't have their stuff" when he faced them. He's a .250 hitter who is going to have good weeks and bad weeks.

Lucky for you (and Janelle) selling is not the same as batting in the Major Leagues. Filling your day with the right activities (the moneymakers we'll explore in a later chapter), assuming everyone is a buyer who wants to buy today, and being dissatisfied with a record performance are all the Janelles of the world need to continually have record months. (Of course, Janelle will also need you to constantly instill these in her.)

Feather or Rocket

Sales management is not like powering a rocket into space; though, many unsuccessful sales managers look at it this way. Getting a rocket into orbit requires tremendous energy expelled in only the first few minutes of the journey. NASA's space shuttles, for example, reached orbit in under nine minutes.

If sales management was like getting a rocket into orbit, you'd work really hard for the first nine minutes, and then your job is essentially done. This is the rah-rah meeting at the beginning of the day, week, or month.

Nine minutes of bluster and then just sit back satisfied and watch the sales come in. But, of course, they never do. Your team never breaks too much above average; and when they do, they eventually regress to the mean. You failed to constantly instill in your team those things that separate top sellers from the rest.

Sales management is more like keeping a feather in the air.

If you've ever done this, you know it takes constant effort; constant blowing on the feather as it descends. Each time you push the feather to a good height, you're (mildly) satisfied… though only for an instant, as the feather is not going to reach some orbit and stay aloft. You know it's going to require constant, never-ending force from you to stay afloat.

Dissatisfaction

Your job as a sales manager is to drive your team to excel. Every day, week, month, and year. Satisfaction after a terrific result, therefore, is great for an instant. But basking too long in the moment – or worse, thinking your job is done – ensures the feather will fall to the ground.

Your future sales results suffer because you stopped blowing on the feather.

A dissatisfied sales manager never stops blowing on the feather. They celebrate the wins and then get right back at it. They use the wins as examples of how much their team can achieve if they keep working to gain those wins; and then they set higher goals.

In our Janelle example, a dissatisfied sales manager would challenge Janelle to sell 25 this month even though 23 was Janelle's personal best. Once Janelle was convinced she could hit 25, her dissatisfied manager would ensure she continuously worked on the right activities, treated everyone as a buyer who wanted to buy today, and that 23 wasn't good enough for this month… the new goal is 25.

Finally, and probably most importantly, dissatisfied sales managers in automotive retail do this on the very first day of the new month – and every day after that. Conversely, satisfied sales managers might challenge Janelle to set a goal of 25 for this month, but they're unlikely to ensure she keeps on pace for this result until around the 29th of the month. Of course, by then it's too late. Janelle has twelve units on the board with two days to go.

…

KEY LEARNINGS:

- Satisfaction – if left unchecked – leads to average performance.

- Your job is never done. What you do every minute of every day is more important than the nine minutes you spent "motivating" your team on Monday.

CHAPTER EXERCISES:

- Evaluate your team and identify those you believe are performing the worst compared to their current abilities/opportunities. What can you do to move these sellers from average to good; and then from good to great? Build a quick plan and start achieving it, with the understanding that this is not a nine-minute endeavor. (Working with those sellers who have the greatest potential return will provide you and the rest of the team the motivation necessary to positively impact the sales results for the entire organization.)

- Repeat. Every single day for the rest of your working life.

8

MOTIVATION OR FAUXTIVATION?

So far, I've written a little bit here and there about motivating your team. I realize, of course, that not every reader will understand fully what that means.

Motivation is an amorphous term; it means so many different things to different people. Motivation is also situational. What motivates one person in one situation won't work in another. For example, as I learned in Marine Corps boot camp, recruits are most often motivated by some combination of fear, peer pressure, and self-esteem to push themselves harder than they ever thought possible.

In the Marines, even after boot camp, fear (of punishment) and/or peer pressure were often effective motivators for those few who didn't embrace the esprit de corps felt by the majority of Marines. Of course, when you put those lacking an esprit de corps – that is, lacking a sense of pride and loyalty – on a sales team in the civilian world, good luck trying to motivate them by fear or peer pressure.

Top sellers won't work for a manager who prefers the stick (punishment) to the carrot (reward); and sales for both successful and unsuccessful salespeople is almost never a team sport. In other words, fear and peer pressure are lousy motivators in the real world.

Fauxtivation

Forgive the negative coaching here, but unsuccessful sales managers often think they're providing motivation when, in fact, they're delivering fauxtivation. That is, fake motivation.

Fauxtivation is delivered sporadically – generally after a bad day, week, or month. It's delivered as either threats or hollow inspiration. It's insincere; and this insincerity is obvious to everyone… except the manager, of course. Fauxtivation is how unsuccessful sales managers attempt to "fire up" their teams.

Even when it works, fauxtivation is like a sugar high; it's ultimately unhealthy and the effects dissipate quickly. Conversely, true motivation is like exercise; the benefits are healthy and long lasting.

Here are some quick examples of fauxtivation to help you recognize this in your own behavior. Fauxtivation is…

> … any negative sales meeting: "You guys better start … or else …!"

> … morning rah-rah sessions without day-long, week-long, and month-long follow through.

> … framed motivational posters in the breakroom or salesroom.

> … motivational memes posted on social media.

> … a written warning for performance.

While I don't want to spend too much time telling you what not to do, I do want to address the last point above. When you are forced to provide a written warning to a salesperson – because they're not performing at an acceptable level – this often means you are the problem.

Did you make a bad hire? Did you fail to train and develop him or her? Did you set the wrong expectations? Did you allow mediocrity? Did you not care if he or she succeeded? Were you inconsistent?

When a sales manager is forced to take punitive action for poor performance, it's nearly always the result of one of the failings listed above. The best way to look at this is that unless you inherited a bad hire, it's always your fault… and that's great news because it gives you a roadmap to avoid these issues in the future.

Motivational Posters are Bad?

Feel free to cover your walls with motivational sayings and images… just believe it, reinforce it, and live it. The same is true for motivational memes on social media. Post away; just be sure you believe what you post, you reinforce what you post, and you live it every day.

Attempts at motivation that are not part of your DNA are meaningless. Good salespeople are good because they can read people. Newsflash: this means they can read you!

Motivation that works comes from your genuine desire to help your team succeed. More importantly, it's your genuine desire to *individually* help each *individual* salesperson succeed. I emphasized the individual requirements of your desire because without wanting (and helping) each *individual* salesperson to succeed, you will forever be mired in mediocrity.

Believe it or not, there are sales managers who want their *teams* to succeed, but care little about more than one or two of their sellers. In fact, these sales managers are secretly pleased when others – even those on their own team – fail.

A German word I mentioned earlier, schadenfreude, best describes these managers. A mash-up of the words schaden (harm) and freude (joy), schadenfreude means deriving pleasure from another person's misfortune. And while you may never have heard the word, we've all met sales managers who seem to take pleasure when a member of their own team fails.

Motivation is Personal

There's nothing wrong with a rah-rah sales meeting. In fact, successful sales managers use these weekly (some even daily) to review best practices, celebrate wins, and reenergize their teams. However, for successful sales managers, the motivation doesn't end when the meeting adjourns.

Successful sales managers continuously motivate their individual sellers. And because they understand their own success is tied to the success of their sellers, they avoid the "tough love" approach so many unsuccessful managers employ. Instead, they treat each interaction as an opportunity to improve performance, even when – or especially when – this means repeating a lesson they've already provided an individual seller… and repeating it… and repeating it… and… You get it.

Conversely, tough love managers revel in their self-righteousness. They provide a lesson once (or sometimes not at all – just expecting good salespeople to already know it), and then they let nature take its course. They feel good about their efforts, and they're quick to tell you they "tried with that guy… he just doesn't get it."

If you get nothing else from this book, internalize the two quotes from the epigraph:

> *"The good news is that if salespeople always did what we wanted them to do, we never would've invented sales managers. The great news is this means you only need to train and reinforce best practices every single day for the rest of your working life."* – Me

> *"If the world were perfect, it wouldn't be."* – Yogi Berra

This training and reinforcement you're tasked with for the rest of your working life, coupled with a desire to help everyone succeed *individually*, is what provides the motivation your sellers need to achieve beyond their own ambitions.

Oh... and the minute you think you've perfected everything, realize you haven't.

...

KEY LEARNINGS:

- Fauxtivation is short lived.

- Real motivation is provided when you genuinely want each individual seller to succeed.

CHAPTER EXERCISES:

- Pick the "worst" seller on your team. Not necessarily the lowest performer, but the one you like the least (or actually dislike). Start today and spend most of your time and efforts for the next week giving your best efforts to genuinely help this salesperson succeed.

- Take what you learn from this week of extra effort and apply it across all your sellers (albeit in an abbreviated form) every single day for the rest of your working life.

9

THE BLAME GAME

Let's level set right from the beginning of this chapter: It's not about you. You are support, and they are sales. Salespeople create all the value for your company. You are an expense. Despite your lofty title, you're no different than the admin clerk who processes sales orders and other paperwork. Your responsibilities may be greater, but your role is the same: Support the sellers.

As I wrote in the first chapter, successful sales managers take the blame when (in the rare instance) their team misses a goal; and they give all the glory to their sellers when they exceed these.

The opposite is, of course, the never-ending finger-pointing that will drive great sellers to work elsewhere and turn your good sellers into unhappy, mediocre timewasters.

Take Blame...

Regardless of the facts, begin accepting the blame for everything that fails to go according to plan, for every goal your salespeople miss, and for every sale your team didn't close. When you do this, you're better equipped to uncover the real solutions needed to grow.

Think about it. As humans, we're hardwired to *not* take the blame for failures. We're hardwired to be victims, if you will, to the actions (or inactions) of others. When things go awry as sales managers, it's human nature to believe it's something outside our control. It's human nature to believe it's not our fault.

But it is your fault. It's always your fault. This is why you make the big bucks.

With the title of manager comes the responsibility to drive results today and, in the future, regardless of the market, the competition, or the team you've been given to lead. When you point the blame of failure on anything or anyone other than yourself, you tolerate the failure because, well, it's not your fault; it was something outside your control. Unsuccessful sales managers use the blame game to make themselves feel better about missing a goal. After all, "I did everything I could do to increase sales, but…"

Unfortunately, this prevents them and their teams from improving. If it's not your fault, there's nothing to fix, right?

By accepting the blame you'll begin to see where the real obstacles lie and, more importantly, how and what to change to remove these obstacles this month and forever. Additionally, accepting blame has a tremendous impact on those above and below you on the organizational chart.

When you accept the blame for a missed goal, for example, and relay this and your plans for improvement to your boss, he or she gains confidence in your ability to lead. When you blame others, your boss only sees you as an excuse machine.

Here's a hint: Owners, general managers, company presidents, etc. don't want excuses, they want solutions. Accepting the blame and formulating a plan for improvement is seen as a solution because it is a solution.

For your team, accepting the blame builds trust in your sellers. Your great sellers understand that if they ever screw up, you'll have their backs. Your good sellers begin to see you as someone who only wants what's best for the team, making them more willing to work harder for you in the future.

As we'll touch on a few times throughout this book, people sell with their hearts and minds, not their backs. You can buy their backs, but you must win their hearts and minds. Pointing your finger at others is the quickest way to lose their hearts and minds.

Of course, there's nothing about taking the blame that's meant to let your underperformers off the hook. Accountability is the foundation of successful sales teams; and if you're genuinely doing everything you can to help someone succeed but they're proving to be incorrigible, feel free to explain to them, "You're not a bad person; you're just not a fit for our team," as you show them the door.

…and Give Praise

Congratulations, your team just had a record month! You worked long hours training and motivating your salespeople last month. You spent extra time with your underperformers, and you helped most of them record their best month ever. Your top sellers also set personal records after you made sure they had no obstacles to impede their growth.

You. Did. A. Great. Job! You genuinely deserve all the praise your boss will be heaping on you.

Deflect it. Deflect it publicly. Ensure your boss knows and your team knows it was the efforts of Bob, Mary, Jeff, and Janelle that led to the record month. Ensure everyone knows your salespeople worked hard to improve their results, and that their efforts paid off.

Loudly give all the praise to your sellers – individually and collectively.

When you do this (and mean it), you'll enjoy a greater sense of self-worth because you increased the self-worth of others. It's a crazy dynamic, but the more you give, the more you get. For truly successful sales managers, heaping praise on others becomes addicting. The more you do it, the more you want to do it.

For your team, they'll not only like you, they'll respect you. They will be infinitely more likely to try harder tomorrow because of what you did today. (More on like and respect in the "Like or Respect" chapter.)

"Yeah, but I want my boss to know how hard I worked, too!"

Believe me, everyone knows how hard you're working. They always know. (Conversely, no matter how much you cover it up with busy work, they also know when you're slacking off.) However, when a business owner, company president, general manager, etc. sees the humility that comes with deflecting well-deserved praise onto others, their respect for you grows exponentially.

…

KEY LEARNINGS:

- It's not about you.

- Take blame – especially when it's not your fault.

- Give praise – even if you did all the work.

CHAPTER EXERCISES:

- Today, and then for the rest of your working life, find a mistake, missed goal, or blown sale that was not your fault, and publicly take the blame for it.

- Today, and then for the rest of your working life, find a success (especially one you drove) and publicly heap praise on someone else.

10

THE TRIAL ATTORNEY

Great trial attorneys never ask a question when they don't already know the answer. They use predetermined questions to lead those on the witness stand to voice the conclusions they want the jury to hear. They are prepared and methodical in their questioning. Anything less and their case would be blown.

Great sales managers, like great trial attorneys, also use questions to lead their salespeople to voice the conclusions they want these same salespeople to hear.

Make no mistake, this is not a cross examination or an interrogation; these are simply questions that drive the results great sales managers want. Questions that lead salespeople to reveal the right answers, rather than always telling them where they screwed up.

Management by Questioning

A friend who owns a successful business once lamented that his sales teams were ineffective selling in the "terrible economy" we were faced with at the time. I was surprised, because this man has always done a great job driving revenue and profit growth through the actions of the great teams he assembled.

When I asked why he thought this was, he said he really didn't know. "It seems I spend hours every day telling my sales managers how to do their jobs, and nothing seems to click," he shared.

Wow! So much had changed for this man and his company since their sales went from slam dunks to half-court prayers. Reread his quote above. What struck me was that this guy used to listen to his sales managers and now he tells them "… how to do their jobs."

You cannot expect to lead by simply telling everyone how to do their jobs.

Listening vs Speaking

I'm hopeful you already understand managers improve their teams by listening, not by speaking. This is an important lesson in leadership development, and it should go without saying. Unfortunately, many in sales management want to be understood so badly, they spend nearly all their time telling and almost no time listening.

Your salespeople know exactly what they need to be successful. The problem for most sales managers is they spend so much time telling, their teams become numb to the constant barrage of "do this; don't do that."

The statistics vary by study, though most people remember about 20% of what they hear. Yet, they recall nearly 70% of what they say. For your salespeople, this means they are about three and a half times more likely to remember the answers they give to your questions than they are the things you tell them.

It's time to perfect the art of asking questions and listening to the answers. It's time to start thinking like a trial attorney and guiding your team to the answers you want them to discover. This is the essence of a Show Me Leader.

And Now, Back to My Friend

So, what advice did I give to my friend – a guy who used to listen and now tells? I provided him five simple questions to review individually with his sales managers daily. Now, when he sits down with them, he "asks" instead of "tells."

1.   What was your team's biggest success today?

2.   Who on your team really stood out and what did they do?

3.   Where does the company have the greatest opportunity in your market?

4.   What are your goals for tomorrow?

5.   How can I help?

I also encouraged him to keep these interactions positive and to refrain from interjecting his opinion. If his sales managers ask him questions, I instructed him to turn these around with his own question: "What do you think?"

Three months into this routine, his team was looking forward to these interactions. They'd turned around their sales, and they were growing market share in a very difficult economy. Over ten years later, his team continues to set records.

Hearts and Minds

This is sales training 101; and we're going to hit this theme a few times in this book: Salespeople sell with their hearts and their heads, not their backs. While you can stand in front of an assembly line worker and "tell" them how to do their jobs all day long, when you interact with salespeople and sales managers, they must buy-in to your vision.

By asking his sales managers questions in a positive manner, my friend was able to make his sales managers think critically about their own teams and markets. When they expressed their opportunities and goals out loud, it led them to work harder to have both a success for today and meaningful goals for tomorrow.

They couldn't wait to share these with my friend. He accomplished all this without demanding they have daily successes and goals; and he also no longer had to tell them anything… he just asks.

Questions for Your Salespeople

If you're managing sales managers, use a version of the questions above – and ask your sales managers to use questions like the ones below with their salespeople daily:

1. What was your biggest success today?

2. What did you do today that really stood out in your mind?

3. Where do you have the greatest opportunity?

4. What are your goals for tomorrow?

5. How can I help?

Remember to keep these interactions positive and refrain from interjecting your opinion. If your salespeople ask you questions, just reply with a simple, "What do you think?"

Of course, like a great trial attorney, you will eventually know their answers before you even ask the questions. However, never stop asking these – even when your team begins breaking records. Be prepared when you begin this daily exercise. Most or even all your salespeople will be a little confused, and some may even just tell you what they think you want to hear. When you suspect this, remember to become the Show Me Leader.

Simply reply, "That sounds great; can you show me?"

You are a trial attorney trying to lead them to the conclusions you would normally express by telling them. Don't worry if it takes time, they'll eventually get there.

...

KEY LEARNINGS:

- Salespeople remember about 3.5X more when they say it than when they hear it.

- Asking questions is a great way to lead salespeople to the conclusions you want them to reach.

CHAPTER EXERCISES:

- Create a list of 3-5 questions you want to ask your team every day that will lead them to express their opportunities, their goals, and their plans for achieving these.

11

SALES CURES ALL ILLS

Sales are up! Great… except… it's a trap!

Most have heard the saying "sales cures all ills," but few understand the meaning. Basically, it implies that so long as sales are good, stakeholders are willing to look the other way on anything not going according to plan.

In other words: If sales are up, it's okay if you and your team suck at everything you do; no one cares… just keep up the good work!

Given this, a more accurate saying might be "sales covers up all ills." When times are good, unsuccessful sales managers care little about processes or rules. This also applies to their "top" sellers. They are growing sales but losing market share and missing incremental deals that deliver even greater profitability than the ones the market grants them.

Beware of good sales, they might be covering up what ails you.

But how would you know if your increased sales are the result of your processes or simply market growth? Well, if you don't know precisely why your sales are up this week/month/quarter/year, then it's the market; and you're likely going to be very sad when the market flattens (or worse).

Good Months and Bad Months

Does this sound familiar?

Your team enjoyed a record sales month – congratulations! Now, fast forward 30 days. The month you just finished was a little more challenging, to say the least. If your response to this was to ask your team something like, "Why were our sales down this month?" then you've got a problem… a big one.

I write that this is a big problem because, of course, you should know. That is, if you knew why your sales were strong a couple of months ago, you would be able to quickly pinpoint why they were sluggish last month.

And therein lies the problem… and the solution.

A good example can be found in retail automotive. Beginning just after the market bottomed (sometime in 2009), virtually all dealers enjoyed growing sales for years as the market grew. Most managers just rode the wave and had zero real clue why they were selling more. Of course, they assumed they were just that good – and their bonuses reflected that.

When the market began to flatten, they scrambled, and they started pointing fingers. Some hired outside companies to conduct sales events for their teams. Quick shot of units retailed.

Some paid for gimmicks to drive unqualified prospects to their floor in search of fabulous (often non-existent) prizes. Quick shot of prospects with a few incremental units retailed.

Most just started throwing money at any vendor who used words like digital, proprietary, in-market, and artificial intelligence in their sales pitch.

Of course, none of these tactics is a strategy, and none is sustainable over the long term.

Why would your sales be down after such a spectacular month in an otherwise flat market? There are plenty of reasons, though the two most common are not mutually exclusive.

First, this could simply be what's called regression to the mean – a mathematical reality I introduced in the "Be Dissatisfied" chapter. In other words, last month you were lucky. You enjoyed lots of good luck. This month, you're lucky too. You're enjoying lots of bad luck. It happens; and it happens to great teams too. The difference is, when great sales teams are hit with a lot of bad luck, they still enjoy good results because their processes endure, and downward swings are minimized.

Second, you may have really pushed last month. Your team "worked" for every deal and you treated every prospect as a qualified buyer who was going to buy today. Then, after breaking your arms patting each other on the back for such a great month, everyone relaxed. You became satisfied. Often, the single greatest difference between great sales teams and those treading water is that great sales teams are never satisfied. They celebrate for about ten minutes, and then they move on.

Process Sells

We know bad habits are created in good times; and in many industries, good times could mean a single month. The key for successful sales managers is they never allow the good times to destroy their good habits; they never allow the good times to dismantle their sales processes.

Process sells. Period. End of story.

Process, however, requires rules. Rules require consequences. Consequences mean accountability. Though accountability doesn't mean punishment. It means accountability… always. In bad times and good.

Sales managers growing market share don't relax their accountability when times are good. And, because they don't, they continue growing share when times are bad. They can pinpoint why their sales are a little sluggish this month because they know their visitor traffic is down 3.2% and their sales lead-to-show ratio has slipped to 24%. They know which salesperson is struggling to move prospects into the write-up and which one is failing to defend their prices in the showroom.

They know this because they have processes, rules, consequences, and accountability; and they track and measure the important things to ensure they're able to spot opportunities for improvement as the month, the week, or even the day progresses.

When you have a good month in a flat or down market, and you don't know exactly what got you to the top, you won't be enjoying the view for very long.

Predictably, your time up there is about two weeks.

…

KEY LEARNINGS:

- Not every good day, week, month, or even year means your team is maximizing their sales opportunities.

- Regression to the mean affects whole teams, not just individual sellers.

- Don't get lulled into inaction just because sales are good.

CHAPTER EXERCISES:

- Dissect last month's sales results and determine exactly why your results were what they were. If you cannot accurately pinpoint the causes, then you have real issues. If you can pinpoint these reasons, keep the good and fix the bad.

12

BE LAZY

If you want to be a successful sales manager, then strive to be lazy. Make no mistake, lazy sales managers are often the best sales managers you'll ever meet.

Being lazy, of course, doesn't mean shirking your responsibilities, letting your team run wild, or napping for a few hours each day in the breakroom. It means being efficient, using your time wisely, letting technology do its part, and managing in real time (so you almost never need to look at a monthly report).

In annoying business jargon, it's shared as, "Work smarter, not harder."

Successful sales managers often do much less "work" than unsuccessful sales managers. While they are indeed working throughout their entire shift, successful sales managers don't waste time on the trivial, they don't have to put out the same "fires" again and again, and they gain efficiencies by driving the actions of their teams (and not doing the work for their salespeople). And, because they're consistent with accountability to assigned tasks and processes, they're not constantly chastising their salespeople to do the basics.

This means they can focus on the longer term and the important tasks that grow sales and profits.

Still don't believe me that successful sales managers do less "work" than unsuccessful ones? Well, let me give you my favorite example of this – something I see virtually every week when working with car dealers.

Successful sales managers in automotive spend little time recruiting, hiring, or training new salespeople. You see, they enjoy almost no negative turnover. Conversely, unsuccessful sales managers often lose entire days and weeks as they are constantly consumed with staffing issues.

I've even had unsuccessful sales managers tell me they can't drive sales activities because they're too busy running ads, interviewing candidates, and onboarding new hires. They are in an endless hamster wheel of "work" that produces nothing in the end. They are ones who will tell you they could hit their goals if they could just hire a few great salespeople.

Only, they never do.

Want to be lazy (and successful)? Solve turnover. In fact, if you solve your sales team turnover issues, everything else is a cakewalk.

Solving Turnover

In my second book, *Assumptive Selling*, I wrote a 10,000-word chapter detailing how to solve turnover in America's car dealerships. Of course, regurgitating a 10,000-word chapter here would not make any of this ridiculously simple. You're welcome.

However, because solving turnover is one of the easiest paths to sales success (and to making you a lazy and successful manager), I will briefly share the key learnings from that chapter along with common traits of those sales managers who enjoy almost no negative turnover.

First, let's agree on a truth about sales team turnover: Salespeople – like all employees – don't quit companies; they quit bosses. Poor leadership drives more good people out of sales jobs than all other factors combined.

Sprinkled throughout the lessons in this book, you'll find the detailed steps to solving turnover issues. Yet, because so many sales managers work better from ordered lists, here are the six steps to creating and maintaining a successful sales team that wouldn't dream of quitting (or underperforming):

1. Ensure you have simple, fair business rules.

2. Offer an enduring, fair pay plan. The issue with most sales team pay plans isn't that they change; it's that when they change, they can feel unfair to your best people. Therefore, the goal is to offer a plan your team feels is fair; one that will only change if a major market disruption occurs.

3. Employ reasonable sales processes. I often find the worst performing sales teams have unconscionable follow-up processes with too many tasks loaded in their CRM. This happens because the salespeople skipped some required sales calls; so, their equally underperforming sales manager "solved" this by loading the process with additional calls the salespeople also won't complete. Insanity.

4. Test these reasonable sales processes. Are they repeatable? Will they lead to higher sales, happier customers, and more productive (and efficient) salespeople?

5. Start enforcing your good rules and reasonable processes. You've already agreed they're good and reasonable, so holding everyone (including yourself) accountable to these should be easy and intuitive. (Accountability comes up more than a few times in this book; though, suffice it to say good people like order and great people love structure, while slugs hate having anyone telling them what to do. If you're afraid to hold people accountable, this means you're afraid of the slugs. How does that feel?)

6. Be nice.

As I wrote, salespeople quit bosses, not companies. Therefore, if you provide a fair pay plan, good business rules, reasonable processes and structure (aka accountability) – and all of this is delivered in a courteous manner with real respect for the individuals on your sales team – you'll discover quickly that your best people don't want to leave; and the competition's best people will want to come work for you.

That's really all there is to solving turnover – and I know this because I've seen it successfully employed multiple times.

In the car business, sales team turnover can hover over 100% for many dealerships. However, when these six simple steps are put in place, these same teams quickly see improved sales results while they enjoy stability among their staff.

...

KEY LEARNINGS:

- Because they're not bogged down with mundane or repetitive actions, successful sales managers have more time to focus on the long-term actions that drive results.

- Solve turnover, and everything else is easy.

CHAPTER EXERCISES:

- Be honest about your turnover. If this is an area where you could perform better, stop trying to find perfect people, and start improving the team you have (or the next hire you make). This simply means putting the six steps into practice.

- For the next week, jot down any actions you take that feel like déjà vu. That is, identify those tasks you've done dozens or hundreds of times before. Do any of these bring you closer to your goals? Can any of these be permanently solved? Can any of these be offloaded onto your team? Can any of these be eliminated?

13

WHAT YOU DON'T KNOW

Surely, you've heard the foolishly obvious statement, "You don't know what you don't know." However, while no one will dispute the veracity of that saying, it amazes me how many unsuccessful sales managers think they know everything.

You. Don't. Know. Everything.

Successful sales managers believe this; unsuccessful ones do not. That's why this short chapter is all about opening yourself up to learning new things. You've made the first step by buying and reading this book; it's now time to become genuinely receptive to ideas from others.

Humility

Successful sales managers – as with all successful leaders – are often described as humble. They're the last to take credit for something and the first to give praise. When a successful sales manager boasts about a record month, he calls out the contributions of his team as the reason for the success.

Humility makes you more likeable and approachable. Being more likeable and approachable makes others want to help you succeed. Moreover, these traits empower other people – including your team – to share their ideas with you. (No one wants to share a great idea with a jerk. He just might take it, have some success, and then steal the credit.)

It's great that others want to share their ideas, as genuine humility makes you eager to hear and try new ideas. Because, after all, you know you don't know it all.

The best sales managers I ever met were not only open to the ideas of others, they wanted to hear every one of them. They sought the suggestions from their lunatic fringe right alongside the well-thought-out plans. Successful sales managers know they can learn from anyone – even the newbie who still hasn't completed her first unassisted sale.

In the last century, it mattered less for sales managers to be open to new ideas, as the rate of change in virtually every industry employing salespeople was relatively slow. Today, changes come fast and furious, and those living off natural traffic or relying on marketing to drive their growth aren't even treading water. They might be growing, but they're losing market share.

Read

Beyond what you can learn from your top sellers, your fresh faces, and even consultants, sales managers wanting to dramatically improve results should seek out and read great sales literature.

Successful sales managers are, for the most part, readers. They've read sales classics from Zig Ziglar and Tom Hopkins, as well as leadership classics from Stephen Covey and Dale Carnegie. They also seek out new authors on these subjects.

They highlight or underline passages from these books as they read; and they implement many of the ideas in real time as they work through a given book. They don't need to (or have the time to) read 50 books a year like Bill Gates. They read when they can.

The great news about reading a leadership or sales training book is that you learn more and make greater improvement in your results by attacking it slowly. You can often read just five or ten pages a day, implementing the next day what you liked about what you read, and then read another five or ten pages that next night.

When you grasp this concept, it makes the thought of reading a 400-page book like *Assumptive Selling* much less intimidating; and the practice of reading a book like this one more rewarding.

…

KEY LEARNINGS:

- Successful sales managers don't have all the answers. They rely on others to develop the next great idea.

- Being humble encourages others to work with you and to provide you with ideas that will drive greater results.

- Read when you can.

CHAPTER EXERCISES:

- Buy a leadership or sales book on Amazon right now. When you're finished reading *Ridiculously Simple Sales Management*, commit to reading 5-10 pages a day of the new book, and implement tomorrow what you read (and like) today. (If you're an automotive sales manager, I selfishly recommend you start with my book, *Assumptive Selling*.)

14

YOU ARE THE TEACHER

I don't know the dynamics in every industry, but in automotive retail, owners and general managers are quick to overpay for outside sales trainers. Too quick, if you ask me... and I make my living as an outside trainer and consultant in automotive.

Certainly, there are times when a company should consult outsiders for sales training. For example, if you purchase a new CRM or other sales-related technology, you'll likely need to pay to have the vendor send someone to train your team. That makes sense.

Additionally, if your company has decided to implement a completely new selling system or methodology – like consultative selling or solutions selling – you'll likely not have the expertise for these on your staff, so you bring in an outside expert. That makes sense.

Finally, companies will often pay to bring in leadership or customer experience experts to help their sales management and other teams drive better results for the company. Again, these are skill sets you'll likely not find on your existing team. That makes sense.

This Makes No Sense!

Not the case in automotive retail. The bulk of the sales training occurring in this industry consists of traveling sales trainers, video training subscriptions, and antiquated sales literature with workbooks sent monthly to dealerships that contain lessons most automotive sales managers could teach in their sleep.

What's worse is that the lessons provided are largely identical to the same training the dealership paid for last year, and the year before that, and the year before that, and the year...

You get it. It makes no sense.

Having delivered much of this training, I can tell you there's virtually nothing I teach salespeople that their sales managers shouldn't already know. After all, every sales manager I ever met in the car business was once a salesperson. Did they have their memories wiped clean by a *Men in Black* neuralyzer when they got promoted?

You might argue I bring a fresh perspective or new methods – which are true – though, these would justify bringing me in once to train a sales team. During my training, an owner or general manager should expect their sales managers to learn these perspectives and/or methods, internalize them, reinforce them with the existing team, and train new hires on these.

One might even expect the sales managers to learn (as I did) and teach these on their own to completely bypass the expensive training I provide.

I'm Not a Trainer

I was once hired by a dealer group to conduct leadership training for their sales managers. During a session, one of their managers made the most amazing and naïve statement I think I've ever heard come out of a sales manager's mouth.

We were discussing how to drive improved results, and this manager had the nerve to tell the group, "I'm a manager, I'm not a trainer."

Yikes!

It took me a moment to process what I'd just heard, as it was truly a bizarre statement for a sales manager to make. Moreover, the manager's boss and boss's boss were in the class.

As the sales manager, you are not only the trainer, you're the primary support, the advocate, and the conduit to everything in your company for your sellers. It's your job to get the best out of each salesperson; and if this means nose wiping, boo-boo kissing, or training, so be it.

If you're not willing to train, then they don't need you.

Overcoming Objections

The bulk of sales training provided by managers in automotive retail centers around overcoming objections and closing. And while these are certainly important skills in the world of selling, the over-focus on these misses the bigger picture of what it takes to turn a marginal performer into a superstar.

It's not about overcoming objections; it's about never having objections. Most sales, regardless of industry, are won or lost during the first third of your road-to-the-sale. Additionally, with the vast amounts of information available to today's buyers, most objections salespeople face today are self-inflicted wounds. (That is, they're creating the objections because they're not focused on the customer's wants and needs.)

Moreover, if your sales team isn't getting in front of enough prospects, then focusing on closing techniques or overcoming objections is wasted effort. Today, success in sales comes from attitude and activity, not from slick word tracks or cool closes.

What to Teach

You've probably seen boards or posters displaying the *ten things that require zero talent*. In fact, you may be among those who posted these in sales areas and breakrooms. Most often, the list posted includes being on time, work ethic, effort, body language, energy, attitude, passion, being coachable, doing extra, and being prepared.

There's nothing wrong with posting this or something similar where your team will see it. In fact, I recommend it. However – and this is what separates the successful from the unsuccessful – these ten things also apply to you. Plus, unless you live these ten, your team will not.

I've witnessed unsuccessful sales managers roll in fifteen minutes late, groggy, unprepared, passionless, and with a crappy attitude. These same managers then spend the bulk of their day being right and having all the answers. They expect their salespeople to embody the *ten things that require zero talent*, yet they demonstrate none of these.

Instead of teaching, they tell.

Your sales team takes their cues from you. However, what you say (that is, what you tell them) is less impactful than how you say it and, more importantly, how you live your work life.

They won't be on time unless you're always on time.

Their work ethic will be driven by your work ethic.

They'll give no more effort than what they see you giving.

Their body language will reflect how you treat them.

Their energy level will rise and fall with yours.

Your attitude drives their attitudes.

They'll never be as passionate as you. If you bring no passion to the job, don't expect them to be passionate.

They become coachable when you actually coach them.

They'll do nothing extra if no one appreciates it.

They'll prepare if they're taught to prepare.

Firm, Clear, & Right

Your argument might be, "But Steve, I'm constantly teaching them! In fact, I make sure I'm firm, clear, and right. They just don't want to learn!"

I hate to burst your bubble, but teachers who are firm, clear, and right are ineffective if the students don't like and respect the teacher. We'll address like and respect in a later chapter; for now, let's focus on making your team teachable.

Simply put, if you want your team to absorb the vast knowledge you possess, and to execute your lessons correctly, they must be teachable; that is, coachable. Their capacity to be coachable is directly correlated to how completely you espouse the *ten things that require zero talent*.

So, post the list of these ten wherever it makes sense in your organization. However, don't post it for them… post it for you. You are the teacher; though, unless you bring these ten to work with you every day, your students won't learn a thing.

…

KEY LEARNINGS:

- You are everything to your sales team. This includes being their teacher.

- Their level of coachability is determined by you and your actions.

CHAPTER EXERCISES:

- Introduce and then post the list of the *ten things that require zero talent*. However, when you introduce these, do so with a confession and a promise to your team. Confess that you've not always lived these and promise that you're committed to living these ten every single day for the rest of your working life. Follow this by asking your team to hold you accountable to these ten, then be thankful (not defensive) when they do.

15

THE MONEYMAKERS

"Okay, I'm a teacher; my team is teachable; so, what do I teach them to do?"

You teach them to work their moneymakers. The opposite of moneymakers, by the way, are timewasters. Every marginal salesperson I know is great at the latter, and never completes the former.

Show Me Your Moneymakers

So much of success in sales is tied to activity, that I find it odd when I hear salespeople complaining about their lack of opportunities all while their heads are buried in their smartphones. There is no secret formula for selling; it's pretty simple, in fact.

The most successful sellers I know are the ones generating the most sales-focused activity. In other words, they know they must do something to sell something! Your marginal sellers need to know this, as well. Once they know it, you now only have to reinforce this every single day for the rest of your working life.

Marginal salespeople need to pick up the phone and call that lead from yesterday. They should send a letter or card to a prior customer a week before their birthday. They can hand their business card to the cashier at Burger King and let her know they pay $100 for every referral she sends them.

For automotive sellers, they can walk into the service waiting area and greet their prior customers or grab their smartphone and start a live broadcast on Facebook showing a cool trade the dealership took in yesterday.

They need to do something… anything. They need to complete moneymaking activities, and this is what you should be teaching them to do.

The Slow Start

If you have sellers who can't seem to get their month going until two weeks in, I suspect they're spending most of their time waiting on prospects to come to them. They're standing outside with a crowd of other marginal salespeople and/or they have their heads buried in their phones.

Instead of wasting their time (and their life) with activities that make them no money, what if you could keep them focused on those actions that drive sales? What if you could keep them focused on the activities that make them money?

I call these activities their moneymakers; and the best way I've found to keep sellers focused on those actions that drive sales is to simply ask them to "show me your moneymakers" whenever I see them without a prospect in front of them.

Show You My What?

If sitting in front of a prospect is how a salesperson makes their living, then their goal should be to always be in front of a prospect. This means, when they're not in front of a potential buyer, their only actions should be geared toward getting a butt into that seat in front of them.

As already shared, the activities that drive that butt into that seat are called moneymakers; and whenever they find themselves just standing around with their hands in their pockets, they simply need to pull out their moneymakers.

This means teaching them to take a one-question test:

1. Am I in front of a prospect?

    a. Yes. Great, close the deal.

    b. No. Then pull out your list of moneymakers and choose one of the activities to do next.

Now do it.

What Are Their Moneymakers?

Again, their moneymakers are those activities that drive a butt into that seat in front of them. Once they understand this, they only need to write down these activities – preferably in some logical order of effectiveness – and keep this list with them at all times. I recommend using simple paper and pen; and keeping the list in their pocket and/or on a post-it note at their workstation.

If I was selling cars today, I think something close to this list would accurately represent my primary moneymakers:

- Prepping for an Appointment

- Making Calls (I would probably break this one down further by type of call, etc.)

- Networking (The old-fashioned kind.)

- Posting a Facebook Live Event

- Sending a Letter/Card

So, if I wasn't in front of a prospect, I could keep jawing with the 8-car folks (and go home broke) or I could choose any activity from this list to fill my next 15-30 minutes. Doing the latter, of course, will bring me closer to my next sale.

For most salespeople, they should be able to create a list of a dozen or more moneymakers, provided they genuinely give this enough thought.

They Can Choose Any Activity?

Yes. The great thing about pulling out a "My Moneymakers" list is that they get to choose which activity they feel like doing. If they don't feel like making calls, they don't have to; they can post a live video to Facebook instead. It's their choice.

The key, of course, is to encourage them to do something... anything that takes them closer to their goal of getting in front of a prospect. In the car business, we like to say, "You can't sell an empty seat." Working a moneymaker list drives the required butts into the seats.

...

KEY LEARNINGS:

- Unless a salesperson is in front of a prospect, their only goal should be to get in front of a prospect.

- Creating and using a moneymakers list is one of the simplest ways to help salespeople stay focused on those tasks that drive their success.

CHAPTER EXERCISES:

- Make your next sales meeting a "Moneymakers" meeting. Start by introducing the concept of moneymakers and timewasters. Ask your team to suggest possible moneymakers and keep a running list (on a whiteboard would be best). At the end of the meeting, ask everyone to create their own moneymakers list, on paper, and keep it somewhere they'll easily find it when not in front of a prospect.

- Beginning shortly after the meeting breaks and continuing every single day for the rest of your working life, ask those not in front of a prospect to show you their moneymakers. Ask them which one they're working on now, and sincerely offer your help.

16

DRIVING ACTIVITIES

It would be great if salespeople just worked their moneymakers without your oversight. Heck, it'd be great if sales just happened all on their own. Of course, if they did, we wouldn't need sales managers. The good news is this means job security. The bad news (for some of you, I guess) is that it means you'll have to work to make sales happen.

The moneymaker exercise from the last chapter will help you and your team stay focused on the important activities that drive sales success. However, if you think your team will just write out a moneymaker list and start doing these without your leadership, you are mistaken.

Human nature for most people is to gravitate toward the easy. And as we learned in "The Fallacy of Monthly Sales Goals" chapter, salespeople left alone will do just that. It's easy to play on my smartphone. It's easy to stand around shooting the breeze with coworkers. It's easy to read the news on my laptop.

Of course, none of these will make you successful in sales… or in life.

For most of your sellers, this means you'll be the one driving the activities… every single day for the rest of your working life. (I'm hopeful you're not tiring of this concept, by the way. Successful sales managers embrace the fact that many on their team require constant, never-ending coaching. They see every interaction as an opportunity for improvement. This means if one seller requires more attention than the rest, that's great news! More opportunity for more improvement!)

Activity

As we've already reviewed a couple of times in this book, the two most important factors that lead to sales success are attitude and activity. The critical reason for this chapter is that most everyone on your sales team will need you to be the catalyst for the activities… or the activities simply will not get done.

Look at any true top seller – those who sell twice what the average salesperson in their company sells – and you'll see someone who is always active.

Simply put, if they're not in front of a prospect, they're on the phone, they're writing an email, they're mailing a birthday card, or they're promoting themselves (and generating new business) through other means (traditional networking or social selling, for example).

Unfortunately, most top sellers are anomalies. They're unique blips on the chart of sales results. They're self-driven to succeed and they're never satisfied. They are their own worst critics and they provide their own motivation. Like marathon runners, they get up and practice their craft even when they're already performing at their best, and when their body tells them to stay in bed.

Of course, the average salesperson is just that… average. They'd love to make more money, but they're fine where they are. For the most part, nothing is really ever their fault, and they don't believe in self-motivation (if it means more work). In many ways, they are the couch potatoes of the business world.

For your company to consistently grow market share and profits, you need a team comprised primarily of top sellers. A team of motivated overachievers who are never satisfied. A team that will get up and practice their craft even when they'd rather stay in bed.

A Team of Superstars?

If you desire to field a team of genuine superstars, you have a choice. You can continue to throw time and money at your recruiting and hiring efforts trying to find the anomalies in the sales world, or you can develop the team you currently have into true top sellers.

By the way, the former strategy has never worked over the long term. Why? Because even if you were lucky enough to find and hire a bunch of superstars, average managers will either drive them away or grind them into mediocrity. (Admit it; we've all seen that movie before.)

Naturally gifted performers come equipped with a great attitude and drive their own activities. Your sales team, I'm sad to inform you, is not solely made up of naturally gifted performers. Most on your salespeople are likely average… as is true for most sales teams.

Once you've mastered the attitude checklist we created in the "Attitude is (Almost) Everything" chapter – and infected your team with your newfound positivity – turning your average players into true superstars requires only that you drive their activities… every minute of every single day for the rest of your working life.

The Best Thing You Can Do for Your Team

Driving activities is not the same as running a sweatshop. Driving activities is also not ensuring your team is busy – I mean, everyone's "busy," right? Furthermore, driving activities is not micromanagement.

Driving activities means ensuring your team is constantly and consistently productive, efficient, and effective.

It's not about screaming, "Everybody better make 50 calls today!" It's about making sure they complete their "money" calls for the day; that they're always working on one of their moneymakers; and that they're using their time wisely.

Driving activities is the best thing a sales manager can do for his or her team.

Let me repeat that with some emphasis so you'll know it's important: DRIVING ACTIVITIES IS THE BEST THING A SALES MANAGER CAN DO FOR HIS OR HER TEAM! Period. End of story.

When you drive activities (the right ones, of course), your salespeople sell more, they make more money, their workday goes by more quickly, and you keep them engaged. The opposite? Well, salespeople who are not productive or engaged only think about survival and about how much this place sucks.

Productive and engaged employees, not surprisingly, don't quit.

Leaders Deliver Results Through Activities

Leadership is not about making friends, doing your subordinates' work for them, or having everyone sit in a circle and sing *Kumbaya*.

Leadership is about delivering sustained results through the actions of your team. Of course, it's preferable that everyone is happy about helping you in this quest to succeed – managing satisfied employees makes leading easier – but their constant happiness is not a prerequisite.

Don't get me wrong, employee satisfaction is critical to long-term success. The problem for many sales managers is they associate employee satisfaction with a near zero-rule environment – often afraid salespeople would quit if they enforced even good business rules and processes.

Satisfied employees are not created in a free-for-all, no-rules workplace. In fact, top salespeople want structure and guidance, and average sellers need structure and guidance.

Genuine employee satisfaction is driven by several factors, including money, accomplishment, pride, engagement, company culture, trust (in their boss), and a sense of self-worth. Providing structure (a.k.a. rules) and guidance (a.k.a. driving activities), coupled with a great attitude, can deliver all of these.

If you "live" the attitude checklist presented earlier, you create the right culture, build their trust in you, and give your salespeople a sense of self-worth. Once you begin driving the right activities, you check off virtually everything else that produces satisfied sellers.

Of course, not everyone on your team will progress at the same speed. Many salespeople will take one step back for every two steps forward. It's your job... strike that... it's your duty to keep them moving in the right direction, growing their skill set, increasing their sales, and making them successful.

When sales managers have a great attitude that they instill in their sellers – coupled with being active managers who also drive the activities of their team – great things happen. The greatest, of course, are that turnover declines while employee satisfaction, sales, and profits increase.

Beware Artificial Activity Targets

I get it. I see this in many of the automotive dealerships I work with.

The dealership sold zero vehicles on a Tuesday. Salespeople spent the entire day in the vaping circle or surfing the web. No one was making their calls. To combat the lethargy, someone on the leadership team demanded action. "I want each salesperson making a minimum of 50 calls per day!"

This new target was announced at the very next sales meeting.

But... to prove they were really, really, really serious this time, one of the managers created a document for every salesperson to sign. This "contract" clearly spelled out that if anyone failed to make 50 calls on any day, they'd face severe discipline, up to and including termination!!!

Ooh, scary.

Once this new rule was in place for a week or so, someone on the leadership team noticed the needle wasn't moving. The dealership sold zero on a Tuesday again... but, the CRM showed everyone was making their calls.

Hmmm. Time for a new, new rule!!!

"Two appointments per day! Every salesperson will set two appointments per day! No one leaves unless they set two appointments!"

Guess what the salespeople now show in the CRM? Yep, two appointments each. Of course, because these are fake appointments, the needle still won't move.

But – and this was important to someone high up at the company – the boxes were checked. All is good in the world... even if we're not selling any more than we were before.

Mandating activities via artificial targets is not the same as driving activities. It's also not productive.

Let's say you're my sales manager at a car dealership, and you demand 50 calls per day from all sellers. Does this rule apply to me if I was busy with customers all day and sold four units? Does it apply to the newbie who has no database of customers to call?

Instead of setting an artificial target that invariably requires you to make exceptions, imagine if you just kept everyone who wasn't in front of a prospect productive? That is, what if everyone was working on a moneymaker whenever they weren't actively selling?

With this mindset and strategy, you'll be forced to find productive moneymakers for your newbie to work on – making him or her more successful more quickly. You'll also leave your four-car seller alone today while you focus on the rest of the team not in front of prospects. Soon, you'll have multiple sellers selling two, three, and four units per day. You'll have your team of superstars.

The Trap of "More is Better"

Beyond the artificial activity targets for the number of calls, appointments, or other activities required each day, sales managers should also be careful not to fall for the trap of "more is better" by forcing pointless activities into their sales processes.

See if this sounds familiar: Salesperson received an inbound sales call that did not result in an appointment or a sale. The salesperson forgot to create a future activity in the CRM (perhaps a follow-up call for the next day); and the prospect ended up buying elsewhere because no one ever called them back.

So, you overreacted and created a process requiring ten calls over the first ten days after all inbound calls are logged in the CRM. To be certain your team never missed a similar opportunity, you assigned two of these ten calls to your assistant sales managers.

Your rationale was strong (to you): If the team wasn't going to set and complete a single follow-up activity, then the CRM should assign ten activities!

This is a classic example of the pendulum swinging way too far to one side. Your new ten-call process invariably causes some salespeople to rethink whether they should even enter inbound sales calls in the CRM. Others (including your managers) just ignore or dismiss these phone tasks.

By the way, why would you assign any of these calls to your managers? Managers that cannot get their salespeople to make calls don't usually complete their own assigned calls, do they? Assigning extra calls to these managers often leads to hundreds or thousands of past due activities in the CRM.

Congratulations.

Required Activities vs Quality Activities

Quick rhetorical question: Would you rather your salespeople made 50 garbage calls per day or made 5 quality calls per day? One more: Would you rather they show two appointments each in the CRM or they set one firm appointment that shows and buys?

I wrote "rhetorical" because we all know the answers. In fact, any successful sales manager knows it's not about the number of activities, it's about making sure salespeople complete quality activities – and that they stay productive throughout the day.

It's not about making calls; it's about making money calls.

It's not about setting appointments; it's about getting prospects to show (and to show on time).

It's not about checking boxes; it's about closing deals.

But It's Raining!

Successful sales managers, as we've already discussed, bring a great attitude to work each day. This attitude is essential when driving productive sales activities. Without your great attitude, speed bumps become roadblocks to average salespeople. Roadblocks that provide perfect excuses for marginal results. Eventually, making excuses becomes the norm for a sales team when their manager fails to bring a great attitude every day.

Of course, excuses only become the norm when you allow them. "It's raining." "It's slow." "We need more advertising." Etc.

When you let these excuses linger in the air without immediately addressing them, you're implicitly giving your team permission to achieve mediocrity. After all, it's raining, it's slow, and we need more advertising.

Successful sales managers shut down negative speech and embrace these situations as opportunities… because they are. Successful sales managers use the slow times to drive even more activities. Because, well, everyone has more time to complete these when we're slow, don't they?

Leadership Via Email

Successfully driving activities requires personal, one-on-one communication. While a sales meeting might set the expectations, it's your butt out of your seat practicing Show Me Leadership that successfully drives the activities.

A trait common with tech-savvy, though still unsuccessful sales managers is the notion they can lead their teams and correct behavior through email. I'm not writing about those managing remote sales teams, as communications necessary for the entire team are often sent via email. I'm writing about sales managers sitting fifteen feet from their sales teams – like those manning the sales desk in an automotive dealership – thinking they can change behaviors with a strongly-worded email.

You cannot lead via email.

Firing off a few terse sentences about how "everyone needs to get their act together" or how you need "everyone to start making their calls" does not work.

It. Does. Not. Work.

Trying to lead via email is the information age version of the old-school sales manager who stood at the front of the room screaming at 30 salespeople about how "no one is making their calls!" In those days (and, unfortunately, I still see this approach used today), the unsuccessful sales manager was simply afraid to confront the two or three salespeople who were not making their calls. So, they subjected the entire team to their rant, hoping the two or three offenders would get the message.

These sales managers were weak. They were afraid to lead. If you're trying to lead by email, you're weak; you're afraid to lead.

The problem with leading by email (or standing in the front at a sales meeting berating everyone for the failings of a couple of individuals) is that those who need the most leadership and oversight don't think you're talking about them – or, more commonly, they just don't care. They know this tirade, like all your tirades, will blow over.

Unfortunately, your top sellers often believe you're specifically addressing them with your rant. They're confused as to why you think they're not making their calls. Some of them quit. Some of them fall into mediocrity. Eventually, none of them like working for you. Good luck getting them to complete moneymaking activities.

...

KEY LEARNINGS:

- Driving activities is the best thing you can do for your team.

- Don't create artificial activity targets, just keep everyone productive: If they're not in front of a prospect, they're working on a moneymaker.

- You cannot successfully drive activities via email.

CHAPTER EXERCISES:

- It's easy to get caught up in the minutia when you're running a sales team; therefore, many sales managers need reminders to get up and walk around. Find a solution (a phone app; an Apple watch; etc.) that can gently remind you every X minutes to engage one or more of your sellers. I recommend choosing a non-standard number of minutes (like every 53 minutes) so that you don't become too predictable. ("The boss gets up at the top of every hour to walk around – be sure to look busy!") After a few weeks of doing this, it's likely you'll no longer need the reminder. You will have internalized this behavior and made it a habit. Congratulations; you're now a full-fledged practitioner of something we introduced in an earlier chapter: MBWA – management by walking around.

17

BOX CHECKING

Newsflash: There's a difference between completing activities and *completing activities*.

The Swinging Pendulum

In the last chapter, we examined artificial activity targets and the "more is better" activities trap. Both ineffective approaches are always the result of an overreaction by someone in a leadership role. Most often, it's the sales manager himself or herself that believes the higher targets or task-laden processes will drive better results.

They will not.

The manager's overreaction to inactivity and/or a slow day/week/month – one that causes the pendulum to swing from one extreme to the other – is typical with an unsuccessful sales team. In these cases, the team goes from making no calls to making no real calls. The team goes from setting no appointments to setting garbage appointments.

The pendulum swung, but the needle didn't move.

"So what?" you might say, "At least the salespeople are doing something productive, right?"

Wrong. Artificial activity targets aren't productive, and they're worse than worthless. In fact, artificial activity targets that were intended to drive results often have the opposite effect.

For example, forcing someone to make a set number of calls without providing them an appropriate number of quality prospects is akin to handing someone a phonebook in the 1990s and telling them to start dialing for customers. Salespeople with great potential will leave; those with no potential will stay and simply learn to fake these activities.

It's Called Box Checking

You want production. You want results. Unfortunately, your mandates will get you neither. They do, however, get you box checking.

Box checking is a pointless exercise completed by those who'd rather be doing something else. They're checking a box because you said they had to. They check the box to show they completed a task they didn't complete. By checking the box, they keep you off their backs. Once they get all their boxes checked, they can go back to surfing the web or standing around in the vaping circle.

They show they're completing activities but they're not really completing activities, are they?

To eliminate box checking you must eliminate the causes. Most often, box checking is caused by the assignment of non-money activities. Your process (or demands) dictate a certain number of sales activities (usually outbound phone calls) to prospects who simply aren't in the market for what you're selling.

In some cases, the prospect has already explained this to your salesperson. However, because you subscribe to the old-school follow-up strategy of "until they buy or die," you demand this of your sellers.

Unfortunately (or fortunately), the world has changed. Today's buyers have more knowledge than ever before, and they're not as quick to fall for a slick sales call as they were a couple of decades ago. Additionally, once they tell you to stop calling, texting, or emailing them, you're done. Laws and rules like the Do Not Call Registry, the TCPA, and the CAN-SPAM Act provide stiff financial incentives to stop contacting those who've asked you to stop.

Of course, your sellers never let it get this far. When they're assigned a non-money task, they simply check the box; they show they completed the activity. You either know this and accept it (which is bad) or you have no idea this is happening (which is really bad).

This brings up the other instance that causes box checking: a lack of management oversight. If you aren't inspecting and driving activities, you are indirectly allowing your team to check boxes.

When your marginal sellers can get away with checking boxes on actual money activities, you have little chance to maximize results. If you're not inspecting activities – and actively driving these throughout the day – unsuccessful salespeople will gravitate toward the easy. It's hard to make a phone call; it's easy to check a box.

The issue here is twofold. First, money activities are skipped, which leads to mediocre results. Second – and just as important – you cannot correct poor performance when activities are faked. Your data is skewed by the fake activities eliminating your chance to gain meaningful insight that would help your team improve their results.

If you want to be a successful sales manager, you should strive for Perfect Data.

The Power of Perfect Data

There's some math that's been batted around in automotive retail for decades. Basically, the math goes like this: Make 1,000 quality calls, sell 30 cars. In my experience, this math has always been fairly accurate. Today, with email and texting, the math is likely closer to: Complete 1,000 quality activities, sell 30 cars.

Of course, if your team is box checking, they can easily show you 1,000 (or more) activities. Their sales results will tell a different story. The math doesn't work because you don't have Perfect Data.

Perfect Data matters. And as boring as that sounds, not only does Perfect Data matter, it matters more than the prospect walking into your store right now. In fact, compared to Perfect Data in your CRM, that prospect is worthless.

What is Perfect Data?

Perfect Data is not Big Data. Perfect Data is Small Data. It's the data you can actually use to make meaningful decisions with your business from day to day and year to year. It's the data that only you own; and it's the most important data for every retail business in America.

Let's look at the impact Perfect Data can have on a sales team in automotive retail.

Perfect Data is exactly what the name implies: information that is accurate, up-to-date and (above all else) a true representation of what happened and what is currently happening on your lot. Another way to describe this is that Perfect Data is a comprehensive reflection of every customer interaction in near real time.

There is a broad misconception with America's car dealership sales managers that Perfect Data gets in the way of working a deal or somehow makes the job of being a sales manager harder. The opposite is true. Perfect Data makes every job in the dealership easier.

With Perfect Data you can decide which salesperson is best suited to handle the next lead, call, or prospect and which one needs help getting folks to take a test drive. Without Perfect Data you spend every sales meeting screaming at the entire team about manager turnovers instead of being laser-focused on the two guys struggling the most at getting a manager involved early in their lost deals.

With Perfect Data you know how many calls, emails, and texts each salesperson completed;, how many prospects they spoke to, how many appointments they set, how many of those appointments showed, and how many appointments they sold.

Let's assume you have two sellers who completed exactly 1,000 activities each last month. One sold 30 units and the other 15 units. With Perfect Data you'd know exactly where your 15-car seller needs help. Of course, if your team was box checking last month, you'd have no clue where to start with your underperforming salesperson.

The more perfect your data, the better your decisions and the more focused your training. Period.

Report Fatigue Syndrome

Now that I have you focused on data; I need to warn you about managing via reports. Managing by reports is fine if it doesn't take the place of MBWA and inspecting activities in real time. Additionally, for most of you, you likely already have too many daily, weekly, and monthly reports to review. This means you could be suffering from RFS: Report Fatigue Syndrome.

RFS is real for some sales managers. Moreover, when you get caught up in the minutia of too many reports – and especially reports that don't provide actionable insight – you can lose track of the goal; you start managing *to* the reports instead of *with* the reports.

My advice is to reduce the number of reports that ever reach your desk or inbox to only those that provide actionable insight. For most sales managers, this often means cutting the number of reports they see by more than half and reducing their view of those reports they still see to a simple summary.

…

KEY LEARNINGS:

- Box checking is not the same as completing sales activities.

- Box checking is not harmless. When you allow box checking, important activities get skipped and your data become meaningless.

CHAPTER EXERCISES:

- Build a plan – one you will execute – to remove non-money tasks from your sales processes. For some of you this may take months to complete. Don't be discouraged; every non-money task you remove from a process increases the validity of the money tasks, while also decreasing the likelihood your team will fall into a box-checking routine.

- Reduce the number of reports that reach your desk or inbox to just those that provide actionable insight. Simply put, review each report, and ask yourself, "Does the data in this report help me make meaningful decisions or otherwise take us closer to our goal?" If the answer is no, then simply stop the distribution of this report. Filter it from your email directly into the trash or ask the sender to stop sending it.

- Once you've reduced the total number of reports you review, ask the creator of each report to develop a dashboard or executive summary containing only those data points you must review. You can always take a deeper dive into the data when the summary indicates there is an opportunity for improvement.

18

LIKE OR RESPECT?

I often ask unsuccessful managers from all fields (sales, admin, service, operations) if they believe their team likes them. The response I most often receive can best be described as contempt:

> "It's not a beauty contest! I don't need them to like me; I just need them to respect me!"

For unsuccessful sales managers, it's important to stress your team is not completing the mandatory, must-do tasks. They're not doing the basics, if you will. (If they were, you wouldn't be an unsuccessful sales manager.) If your team is not doing the basics you've deemed as mandatory, what makes you believe they respect you?

Hint: Despite your self-righteous indignation, they do not. If they respected you, they'd complete those tasks you said were important, correct?

Instead of debating whether you're liked or respected, why not be both? Because short of supervising a team of ditch diggers, you cannot enjoy sustained success in management if your team does not both respect and like you.

Hearts and Minds

As I've already written a few times, salespeople sell with their hearts and minds. Therefore, winning their hearts and their minds should be paramount to winning their backs, arms, and legs. Let me explain.

You can certainly ensure everyone on your sales team arrives by 8:00 a.m. When they're late, you can give them a written warning. When they're constantly late, you can terminate them. After all, they weren't cut out for the sales game, were they?

But what if everyone on your team was always on time solely because they were afraid of losing their jobs? What kind of sales environment would this create? Does this mean they respect you?

Of course not. It means they want to stay employed. It doesn't mean they're going to work harder to make deals. It doesn't mean they're going to seek out additional training or read a sales book to sharpen their skills. It doesn't mean they're going to dig deep for additional opportunities.

It just means they're going to show up on time… with a crappy attitude.

When your team likes and respects you, they'll do more because you've won their hearts and minds. And guess what? When you win their hearts and minds, they bring their backs, arms, and legs along for the ride.

Coaching for Likes

Quick question: Which sales manager below do you think is liked by his or her team?

> Sales Manager Joe: When Joe sees a salesperson doing something incorrectly or skipping a sales task, he's quick to tell them what they did wrong. He reminds them that this kind of behavior is not tolerated. He warns them that if they don't shape up, he may have to terminate them.

> Sales Manager Jane: When Jane sees a salesperson doing something incorrectly or skipping a sales task, she weighs the behavior against the goal of maximizing opportunities. If she feels it's a simple mistake, she may say nothing. If it's something else, she offers coaching to the seller with the sole aim of helping that salesperson make more money. No judgement; no stern warning; no "or else."

It's not just that the salespeople working for Joe don't like him, they also don't respect him. Moreover, those who have the potential to be great sellers will either leave or settle into mediocrity. Everyone who remains on Joe's team will do the minimum necessary to keep their jobs.

Conversely, those working for Jane like and respect her. They're less likely to repeat mistakes and more likely to take risks. They'll also do more than what's required; and because they know Jane is invested in their success, they're more likely to be invested in hers.

Have Fun!

Every successful sales team I know has fun. It's a fun place to work, they enjoy what they do, and they like their manager. If this does not describe your sales team, you've got a problem. The good news is you're the only one who can solve it.

As I described in the "Being Dissatisfied" chapter, successful sales management is like blowing a feather to keep it aloft. When your team dislikes working for you or looks at their career with you as just a job, they're not having the kind of fun successful sales teams enjoy.

In the feather example, it's as if the feather is wet when working for you is not fun. Imagine trying to keep a wet feather aloft. It's not possible!

Having fun, by the way, is not the same as chaos; it's not a free-for-all. In fact, with adults it's just the opposite. Having fun at work is about knowing you're appreciated, understanding where the boundaries are, and feeling satisfied with the outcomes. Everything in this book is meant to help you make your work environment something successful people would enjoy. After all, we're not trying to attract and maintain the slugs.

They Are Volunteers

A customer service lesson I teach called "Volunteers and Orphans" is one that will help sales managers looking to create a better work environment that drives results. The idea of "Volunteers and Orphans" is that companies will always provide a great customer experience if they treat their employees like volunteers and their customers like needy orphans.

This approach improves customer satisfaction because it forces management to appreciate the contribution of their frontline employees (as you would if they were volunteers), while ensuring everyone put the needs of customers ahead of their own (as you would if they were orphans).

Why does it make sense to treat salespeople like volunteers? Because they are! They *volunteer* their hearts and they *volunteer* their minds. If you want the best work out of them; if you want them to make great decisions; if you want them to deliver stellar results; then you must treat them like volunteers.

Treating them like volunteers forces you to appreciate their individual contributions.

If you think treating them like volunteers means there's no accountability, you're looking at this the wrong way. Volunteers are not only held accountable, they embrace accountability.

Imagine you are running a charity staffed with volunteers. While you'd be grateful for everyone who volunteered, you wouldn't allow any of these volunteers to circumvent your rules. You wouldn't allow them to steal or to treat others poorly, and you wouldn't keep them on your staff if they were habitually late. In other words, you would have rules and processes in place, and you would be happy to have all your volunteers until one of them breaks your rules. Once they did, there would be consequences.

Of course, because you're happy to have these volunteers and you appreciate their individual contributions, your work environment would be described as fun. And because they know you appreciate their individual contributions and that you're happy to have them working with you in this fun environment, they don't break the rules and they don't circumvent your processes.

Be Nice

I've never understood the screaming manager. Yes, anyone with a brain knows the screaming manager tactics are unsuccessful today; though, I honestly don't know when screaming tactics have ever been successful. As I've already written, great salespeople won't work for jerks… they don't have to; there are too many other opportunities out there for top salespeople – in any economy.

If you are a screamer, why do you feel you need to raise your voice… ever?

When you're really in charge, you don't have to snarl or even look mad. When you're really in charge, you don't have to yell. If you are a screamer, it's time to make a serious change. You can either change your approach or your profession. No one needs a screamer managing their sales team.

…

KEY LEARNINGS:

- In sales management, like and respect go together.

- When your team respects you, they complete the activities you've deemed important.

- When your team likes you, they're invested in your success.

CHAPTER EXERCISES:

- Write the word "VOLUNTEERS" on a Post-It Note and stick it to your desk, desk phone, or computer monitor. For at least the next two weeks, judge all your interactions with your salespeople against this word. That is, am I treating them like volunteers?

19

PROMOS ARE NOT PANACEAS

In the last chapter we learned your workplace should be considered fun for your sales team. In this chapter we'll look at various ways to make it fun with promotions and contests… however, let's first get a mutual understanding on the power and the pitfalls inherent with promotions and contests.

Promos are not panaceas.

Because this book is supposed to be ridiculously simple allow me to translate:

> Promos/Promotions: Spiffs, incentives, contests, bonuses, etc.

> Panaceas: Cure-alls

The best sales contest in the world won't repair a broken culture or make up for a lack of sales processes or drive sustained regular sales activity.

Understanding that sales contests are not cure-alls is important, as too many unsuccessful sales managers often ride from sales contest to sales contest hoping that if they throw enough money at the problem, they'll achieve the desired results. Sometimes these contests help them hit their numbers and sometimes they do not.

Of course, when your results are the product of short-term spiffs, you're building nothing for the future. In fact, you're often mortgaging your future for today's sales. Let me explain.

Let's say you manage a team of nine sellers, and you hold a sales contest this month that pays a crazy amount to your top three salespeople, a good amount to your next three, and a small amount to the bottom three if the team reaches its overall goal. However, you don't manage activities and most on your team don't like you (or don't necessarily like working for you).

All nine sellers will cut corners this month. They'll pull sales from next month into this month. If word about the contest leaked early, I guarantee they sandbagged at the end of last month to pad this month. They'll quickly assess every prospect and throw the "non-buyers" to the curb. (In automotive retail this is called "brooming" – where salespeople "sweep away" the tire-kickers so they can focus on those ready to buy today. It's a lousy strategy that ensures their dealership will sell fewer cars today and tomorrow.)

What they won't do is strictly follow your processes or deliver the activities that drive long-term results. They're focused on this month and only this month. Next month and next year will have to wait. Of course, this means you'll need an equally lucrative contest next month if you expect to continue growing your sales results.

Sales Contests are Good

Don't get me wrong, I like spiffs and contests. Done correctly, these increase employee satisfaction while driving better results… if, that is, your contests don't reward those who circumvent your processes.

It's also important to note that spiffs and contests don't cure anything. If your team isn't making their required calls or following your processes, adding an incentive this month will not help. In fact, it will just make these issues worse. Spiffs will not motivate a team to do the right things when your efforts have already failed to do so.

Successful sales managers employ sales contests to create some good-natured competition, reward their teams, reinforce the behaviors they expect, and have some fun. Any sales incentive you create should do the same; though it should especially maintain the long-term behaviors you want.

Design for the Cheaters

The saying "everyone works their pay plan" doesn't mean salespeople will diligently complete all the assigned sales activities necessary to maximize their pay. It means salespeople will find every shortcut, workaround, and trick they can to maximize their pay.

This doesn't mean they're bad; it means they're human.

Because of this, be certain you design your contests and spiffs with the cheaters in mind. Look for every possible loophole (because your sellers will) and find every possible way you could be conned (because your sellers will), then put the proper structure and rules in place to eliminate these.

Additionally, be wary of the unintended consequences. This means play out the possible scenarios in your head if your team is successful and truly crushes the incentive. I'm sure you're wondering what sort of unintended consequences could be bad if you blow past your objectives (beyond paying out more than you anticipated); let me give you two quick examples just to make my point:

- A car dealer wants more sales appointments because appointment customers are two times more likely to buy than walk-ins. To entice the team to set more appointments that show, the dealer pays a $50 spiff for each legitimate appointment that shows on Saturdays this month.

  Two unintended consequences result. One, the sales team no longer sets Monday appointments on Mondays. Instead they ask everyone, "What time *Saturday* works for you?" (Appointments in the car business set for five days away rarely show up.) Two, Saturdays were already the dealership's busiest day of the week. Now – because of so many appointments – walk-in guests are ignored, and the sales stay flat (or worse) for the month.

- A food and beverage distribution company needs to get a 20% increase this month to finish the quarter strong. They create a volume bonus for their sales team that pays a big spiff if they can achieve 120% or more of their individual goals.

  Salespeople unload excess product into the backrooms of their customers who will allow it (or who won't notice it). This creates an oversupply situation the following month that depresses those month's sales. Additionally, because much or all of what they sell is perishable, the distribution company ends up crediting many of their accounts a few months later for the stale product.

While those scenarios might seem unlikely to you, I've witnessed these exact situations (and dozens like them) firsthand. In neither of these did the salespeople cheat… they just worked their pay plans while their companies paid out big bonuses that failed to achieve the desired result.

Let's Make it Fun

So, how can we make it fun to be on your sales team? Spiffs, contests, and incentives should be fun, after all.

Given that every industry is a little different, many of these sales promo examples may not apply to you. The rationale for this list is to give you ideas you can incorporate into your business. However, before I list the ideas, we should detail some manager expectations before, during, and after any sales promotion you run.

Before Every Promo

Prior to announcing any sales incentive, it's critical sales managers cover a few bases to ensure the incentive will drive the desired short-term and long-term results. Specifically:

- Did you design it for the cheaters? If not, review the possible loopholes now.

- Will it be fun? If not, start over.

- What's the potential financial/sales impact during the contest period and in future weeks/months/years? In other words, will this incentive just juice sales for a short time or will it also drive the behaviors you want over the long term? Will it just pull ahead future sales, or will it indeed increase sales today and in the future? If the team maximizes their results, can the company afford to pay out the maximum?

- Keep the contest a secret! Unless you want your team sandbagging at the end of this month, don't release any details of next month's incentive until the first day of the contest.

During Every Promo

Unsuccessful sales managers are famous for creating incentives and then either using a set-it-and-forget-it strategy or changing the rules as the month goes on. While both will guarantee your sales incentive will not achieve the desired results, the latter also causes good salespeople to quit.

I assume you created the contest because you wanted to motivate/reward your team while also driving better results now and over the longer term. To do this, you've got to stay abreast of the results and engaged with your team throughout. Specifically:

- Keep score in near real time. No one on your team should ever have to guess where they stand at any given moment during the incentive; plus, scoreboards have a way of motivating everyone to do more.

- Encourage constantly. Your sellers should see your primary goal as helping them individually succeed in sales. When they do, they're more likely to do the extra work necessary to exceed their goals.

- Challenge constantly. Beyond encouraging everyone individually to maximize their results during the incentive, be sure to also challenge those you know could be performing better.

- Stoke fun rivalries every day. Remember, working on your team should be fun. Contests are a great way to drive performance while also having fun. There are already friendly rivalries on any successful sales team, so be sure to leverage these during your incentives.

- Be the checks and balances. Despite your best efforts to design a cheat-free incentive, if you wait until the contest is over to inspect the results, you're likely to pay for some cheating.

After Every Promo

To get the most out of every incentive, successful sales managers openly celebrate the top performers, as well as their entire team. And while they don't let last month's success cause a slow start to this month, they do a bit more than just hand out the bonus checks after a successful sales incentive. Specifically:

- They give all the credit to their team when the goals of the incentive were exceeded and take all the blame when not.

- During their celebration meeting announcing the final results and handing out the checks, they provide an analysis of the high points and the low points of the contest. Done right, this summary can create a nostalgic reminder of the incentive in the minds of the sellers while also driving home the best practices and other behaviors the sales manager wants to instill.

- They ask those above them on the organizational chart to also congratulate the team (as a group and individually as they see them) using specific data from the incentive. (For example, "Hey Bob, great job last month – thirty-five is a new personal best for you, isn't it?")

A Few Ideas...

Running the same incentive month after month is a sure way to take the fun out of sales contests. If it's a winner-take-all event (like salesperson of the month), you often get the same three or four sellers trading honors throughout the year. If it's a lucrative volume spiff, you'll notice most sellers hit the bonus about every other month. That's because they sandbag in one month and pull ahead in the next.

The trick for you is to find ways to keep your sales contests fresh and fun, while ensuring these drive the behaviors you want over the long term.

Salesperson of the Month – There's nothing wrong with awarding someone on the team the salesperson of the month honors. In fact, I strongly recommend it. Sales is not youth soccer; no one is getting participation trophies. In sales there are winners; and these winners should be celebrated loudly and clearly.

However, just be sure this isn't the only sales contest, incentive, or promotion you run. If it is, be prepared to have more than half the team lose interest.

At the very least, winning the salesperson of the month honors should include a bonus check and the salesperson's name on a plaque. Highlighting their accomplishment on the company's social media accounts is a nice add, as is a prime parking space (where this makes sense).

The Odd Trophy – As part of or in addition to the salesperson of the month honors, consider creating an odd trophy that fits with your industry. When I ran sales for a large Budweiser distributor in the 1990s, we created a Budman trophy using a Budweiser Budman tap handle. We presented this odd trophy to our salesperson of the month to display on their desk throughout the following month.

Be creative with this. For example, the odd trophy doesn't have to have anything to do with your industry. I've seen sales organizations get their hands on a decades-old, large, hideous bowling trophy to pass between winners.

Nothing says the winner of the odd trophy must be the salesperson of the month either. I recommend creating a different monthly spiff (that focuses on something important to your company that month) to determine the odd trophy winner. This way, all salespeople have a chance to win, creating even more competition.

Champions Belt – Similar to the odd trophy, this one involves a prize that rotates among the team. Just buy a custom-made championship belt (like they use in professional boxing) and present it to the winner each month. Like the odd trophy, they'll take pride in displaying this all month long.

Prize Wheel – Prize wheels are excellent motivators on a budget, as the wheel is usually loaded with inexpensive items (like gift cards or delivered lunch), and one bigger prize (like cash). These become motivational when the winners spin the wheel in front of the rest of the team. Prize wheels are versatile and work great for regular incentives or ad hoc spiffs (explained next).

Ad Hoc Spiffs – These are fun, quick (usually a single hour, day, or week) contests that sometimes also involve a fun activity. Ad hoc (which means "when necessary") spiffs are often a great way to drive excitement and activities during a slow day or week. Ad hoc spiffs are most successful when the rules are clear, and the timeline is relatively short.

For example, let's say you're a sales manager at an RV dealership. For your team, Tuesdays and Wednesdays are probably relatively slow days, which makes these days perfect for quick, ad hoc spiffs. Successful spiffs I've seen used in these situations include rewarding for same-day appointments.

Announce the spiff first thing in the morning; awarding a spin on your prize wheel for every same-day appointment that shows. Award a second spin if the shown appointment results in a same-day sale.

A word of caution: Ad hoc spiffs work best when they are infrequent and unpredictable. If you always spiff for same-day appointments on Tuesdays and Wednesdays, then your team will start to force their appointments into those days; hiding these appointments until the morning of the spiff, then magically "setting" these appointments that morning to qualify.

Power Hour – Sales managers have used some version of power hours for decades. Generally, these are designated times when the sales team focuses on outbound call activity. Unsuccessful sales managers often think creating an ongoing power hour will solve their inability to drive sales activities. Hint: these do not.

If you aren't successful at driving activities consistently throughout the day, setting aside one hour where "everybody better start making calls" is foolish. Your power hours will last a few days, then everyone will realize you weren't serious (again), and they'll go right back to whatever timewaster they were doing previously.

Power hours are often employed successfully as ad hoc spiffs when a clear, targeted goal is laid out. For example, dropping an unannounced power hour into the middle of the day that awards prize wheel spins for contacting previously unsold prospects and getting them to commit to a return appointment can be a fun way to generate some of the most dreaded calls salespeople are tasked with making.

F F & F – For sales teams who sell directly to consumers (Realtors, automotive salespeople, etc.) using Facebook and other social networks is a terrific way to generate leads and sales. Moreover, when a prospect connects with you on/through social media, they often trust you like a friend – making these easier and more profitable deals for your salespeople. Of course, this makes the need to build an audience important.

For this incentive, you're going to pay for Facebook Friends and Followers. Start with a baseline for all sellers (this means getting a friend and follower count for each salesperson) and create two prizes. One for the most friends and followers added and one for the greatest percentage increase in these. This incentive works best as a monthly contest, though be sure to create strict rules to stop cheating. Fake friends and followers can be bought, so only count those who live in your market.

Weighted Teams – A weighted teams incentive work great to improve the skill set and activity completion of your underperforming salespeople. The concept is simple: rank your sellers based on last month's results, then pair the top seller with the bottom, the second-best seller with the second worst, etc. The winners this month are the team that shows the greatest improvement over their previous month's total.

Formal Teams – If your salesforce is already divided into teams (or if it makes sense to do so), setting up incentives that pay for overall team improvement are a great way to engage and motivate your below average sellers via assistance delivered by those on top.

No "I" in Team – In this case, the I stands for Individual. In this contest, the entire team either wins or loses. Team-wide incentives can be simple – if we sell X, everyone is awarded Y – with the rules easy to write and the results easy to track and measure.

The "I" in Team – This is a slightly more complex version of the team incentive. In this case, everyone must individually reach their own goal for the team to bonus. By tying the overall bonus to the performance of each seller, you drive both team and personal performance. For most sales teams, this also creates a dynamic where your successful sellers drive better performance from your bottom dwellers in a productive way.

Five Card Sales Stud – Like traditional five card stud, this one is a poker contest. Unlike regular poker, however, this one awards a card to each of your sellers as they complete different goals throughout the month.

The trick is they can only keep five cards at any time, so once they reach five cards, they need to discard one of these five before they get to draw a card for their most recent achievement. Certainly, they can stop drawing at any time and keep their five cards.

At the end of the month, they compare their hand to your payout chart (based on actual poker hands) and receive their bonus. (Depending on the size of your team, you may need to have multiple decks. Additionally, eliminate any urges to swap cards with others by keeping everyone's current hands posted for all to see.)

Beat the Manager – This is a fun ad hoc spiff that can fire up the team during and after this quick contest. For this incentive, you join your team in a sales activity (usually phone calls) for a specified period (generally one or two hours).

If you chose phone calls as the sales activity, for example, you could tally points based on the following criteria: One point for every prospect you speak with and two points for every verified appointment set. Each salesperson who beats the manager's total points wins a grand prize (two spins of the wheel, for example); those who tie the manager win a second prize (one spin of the wheel in this example).

Target Transaction – Usually a one-day or one-week contest, this one is simple. You pick a target prospect randomly for each seller. The first salesperson to close their deal wins.

March Madness – Get beyond how cliché or how overdone you think this one is, as bracket challenges managed correctly drive incredible results, while also keeping everyone motivated all month long. Start by creating a bracket like the NCAA tournament, though be sure to add a consolation bracket and something I call The Bucket. Depending on the size of your team, each challenge may last a few days or an entire week. Also, there's no rule against running your bracket challenge incentive for longer than a month.

If you can, set a different challenge for each step in your brackets (volume-only incentives can get predictable and boring), and have some smaller payout for each head-to-head win. When someone loses a head-to-head contest, they're moved to the consolation bracket. When they lose twice, they're dropped in The Bucket. Those in The Bucket also compete in the same challenges as those still in the two brackets, and each challenge winner from The Bucket also receives that challenge's small prize.

The grand prize is awarded to the winner of the main bracket, second prize is awarded to the last loser in that bracket, and third prize goes to the winner of the consolation bracket.

Real Sales, Fantasy Football Style – This one takes some planning, but if you've ever played fantasy football, you probably can imagine how involved a head-to-head incentive based on scoring different criteria can be.

For this contest, you need to schedule your salespeople to go head-to-head each week against a different seller. Additionally, you'll need to add some scoring metrics that reward points based on performance. For example, every phone call made is worth 0.1, every phone call connected is worth 0.5 points, every appointment show is worth 3 points, and every sold customer is worth 7 points.

You simply track these throughout the week and award a win (and some small bonus) to each seller who beats their head-to-head competitor at the end of the week. Do this for the first three weeks of the month. During the fourth week, the top two (or more, if multiple sellers have the same record) compete for the grand prize and a consolation prize using the same criteria you used in prior weeks.

PB & J – Not what you think. This one rewards those sellers who exceed a Personal Best (PB) with a Jackpot (J). Generally, this one works best as an ongoing incentive. To start, create a baseline of each seller's personal best (volume, profit, etc.). When they exceed this personal best, they win the jackpot.

The jackpot can be a set amount, or it can be a progressive jackpot that grows each month until someone exceeds their personal best. If you choose to go the progressive route, you can have a different jackpot for each seller based on how high their personal best is relative to everyone else, and their time with you (you certainly don't want to award a newbie in his third month the same amount you would award a ten-year employee who breaks her own long-standing record month).

Money Machine – If you've got a decent budget for sales contests, you may want to invest in a money machine (money machines are those booths that blow bills around while the person inside tries to grab all they can). Putting this machine at the front of the salesroom and using it for both ad hoc and regular incentives can create a lot of fun and excitement for your sales team.

Big Game Hunter – For most sales teams, it's not just about volume. Sometimes, it's also about how much revenue or gross profit is realized from a given deal. This one is super simple and makes a great ongoing incentive that can also incorporate your odd trophy (perhaps with a hunting theme). The winner each month is the salesperson who bags the biggest prey – whether straight revenue or gross profit. Be sure to track this throughout the month so everyone knows the value of the deal they need to be beat.

Double-Shot Day – This is a fun, ad hoc contest that doubles the normal payout for any deals consummated on the day this is announced. Of course, you never want to announce this incentive in advance – just spring it on your team the morning of your Double-Shot Day.

Post-Meeting Dash – Another fun, ad hoc incentive. Like Double-Shot Day, this one is never announced in advance. Unlike Double-Shot Day, this one doesn't last the entire day, just for a few hours after the meeting breaks. Choose your own targets (calls made, calls connected, verified appointments made, sales made, etc.) and pay the bonuses as soon as the dash ends.

The Raffle – If the same salespeople win most of your contests and incentives, you may want to try the raffle approach. With a raffle, you're still driving and paying for improved performance, though you're giving everyone a shot at the grand prize. Basically, you create the incentive to award raffle tickets based on individual performance; though, the more you sell (regardless of your goal), the more raffle tickets you can earn.

With this approach, your bottom sellers who achieve their goals, but sell fewer than the top salesperson with the huge database, still earn raffle tickets and chances at the larger prizes. Your top seller just earns more chances.

Matching Referrals – If your company pays customers and others for referrals who buy from you, consider running a matching referrals incentive for a month. In this contest, you'll give your seller an equal amount to the referral fees their network generated during the month. This can be a great way to jump start a stale, mostly unused referrals program.

Us or Them – When you have direct competitors who can be easily tracked, running an us or them incentive has been proven to energize and focus your team on the potential to sell even more. Managers in automotive retail have been successfully using this incentive off and on for years, as every OEM posts the MTD and YTD new car sales for dealers in the district, region, and nation. With the us or them contest, you generally pay when your team moves up a spot or two in the district or regional rankings. Us or them is also a great way to increase CSI (where your manufacturer still tracks and ranks this, of course).

Total Profit/Gross – Whatever you call gross profit (in automotive retail it's called gross; in most other industries it's called profit or gross profit), you can add a nice one-week, ad hoc contest that pays the team if your total gross profit for the week exceeds a given amount.

Mana-a-Mana – While the Spanish term mano-a-mano means hand-to-hand, this one stands for manager vs manager. This contest can be run as part of an existing team versus team competition or all by itself to spice up an otherwise dull week or month.

With mana-a-mana, each sales team's manager is competing to win a grand prize and/or not be the manager having to complete some humiliating act for losing. Feel free to get creative with this, as there is almost nothing that helps build more trust and respect for a manager than when the manager allows himself or herself to be humiliated for the greater good.

From receiving multiple pies in the face to standing in front of the store in a hot dog costume with a giant "sale" sign to camping out on the store's roof for a week, I've seen successful sales teams take this one to the limit.

One Last Thought on Promotions

These were just a few ideas to get you started; however, I left out an important point about any type of contest or recognition that you run for your salespeople. That is, think of their significant other!

When we look at top sellers across all industries, one thing holds true almost every time: They dedicate a fair share of their "off hours" to selling more and/or improving their skill set. Because of this, it's important to find ways to involve their wives, husbands, boyfriends, girlfriends, parents, and even kids in your incentives whenever possible.

This might mean designing prizes that would appeal more to their significant other(s) or even inviting these important people in their lives to a celebratory dinner or presentation. Whatever it takes, be sure to always remember that behind every great seller is a personal support staff (parents/spouse/kids/etc.) that also sacrifice to make it all possible.

…

KEY LEARNINGS:

- Running regular and irregular (or ad hoc) sales incentives are a great way to motivate a good team.

- Of course, no matter how good the promotion, it will never cure all that ails a broken team.

- Successful promotions are never set-it-and-forget-it. They require planning and your active involvement before, during, and after the promotion.

CHAPTER EXERCISES:

- Take a hard look at the sales incentives you and/or your company has run over the last twelve months. Did they move the needle for the short term, long term, or both? Did they help create the behaviors you want in your sellers, and did these last beyond the contest? Are you a better team today because of the contest?

- Using what you learned from analyzing past promotions, design at least your next three incentives following the guidelines laid out in the first part of this chapter; paying close attention to what you'll need to do before, during, and after the incentive.

20

BE SATISFIED

Yes, I know I told you to be dissatisfied in an earlier chapter.

Yes, I'm now telling you the opposite. More specifically, I'm telling you to be satisfied with the sellers you currently have on your team.

Not with their performance (unless it's stellar), but rather, be satisfied with them. Be satisfied with the fact that as mediocre as they are now, they are the most likely candidates to be your future trained killers (figuratively speaking). Be satisfied knowing this is what they can become under you.

If you've been applying what you've been reading in this book, then you've already begun to see improvement in your bottom and middle sellers. You also know it's not who you hire, it's how you lead. (In the next chapter, we'll dive even deeper into how to turn virtually any salesperson into a top seller; though, really, that's what this whole book is about, isn't it?)

Too often, unsuccessful sales managers believe if they can just replace the bottom third of their sales team, their job becomes easier. Of course, for these teams, the bottom third has become a revolving door. Unsuccessful sales managers are constantly dealing with turnover issues. So much so, it's hard to focus on leading and training when you're always recruiting and hiring.

So, as the title states… be satisfied. Be satisfied with the sellers you have, because if you're truly becoming a top sales manager, you'll turn bad into good, good into great, and great into true superstars.

…

KEY LEARNINGS:

- Be satisfied with the team you have, as they're your best chance at long-term success.

CHAPTER EXERCISES:

- Find at least two redeeming qualities in each of your current sellers; make these your focal points for the next few weeks. That is, if someone is an average seller but always punctual, start praising him or her for constantly being on time. When you do this, two things happen: One, they begin to feel more confident with their vocational choice – making them better sellers; and two, you begin to genuinely appreciate their redeeming quality – making you more personally satisfied with them and more willing to work hard to make them better.

21

CREATING WINNERS

While all sales managers want a team of true superstars, successful sales managers *build* their teams to become true superstars. Conversely, unsuccessful sales managers obsess over *acquiring* a team of true superstars. So much so, they're constantly looking to replace their mediocre performers in their search for winners. To hear them describe their situation, they're just a few great salespeople away from really crushing their numbers.

But they're always just a few great salespeople away from this, aren't they?

To an unsuccessful sales manager, a true superstar is a naturally gifted, self-motivated, self-sustaining humanoid set on autopilot. If they could include this description in their job postings, they would.

Successful sales managers know (as I've already written), it's not who you hire, it's how you lead. If a successful sales manager is leading a team of true superstars, it's because he or she made it happen – not through recruiting and hiring, but through the very things you're learning in this book.

If you agreed with the direction laid out in the last chapter – that is, that your current sellers present the greatest opportunity for you to enjoy long-term success – congratulations; you've taken a major step in leading a team of true superstars. Now comes the fun part.

Do You Care?

When you genuinely care about the individual success of each of your sellers, you'll quickly learn that leading them can be an enjoyable task… some might even describe it as fun. Motivating those you care about is easy and natural… and honest.

As you learned in the "Driving Activities" chapter, leadership is about delivering sustained results through the actions of your team. Salespeople can only help you deliver sustained results if they maintain the right attitudes and complete the important activities.

When you care about the individual success of each or your sellers, you create the right attitudes and constructively drive the important activities – even among those who would've been considered mediocre under a lesser manager.

When you only care about your numbers, you stunt the growth potential of your entire team and can even drive away those few sellers you hired that you believed were true superstars.

Sales is a Numbers Game

Certainly, you've heard sales described as a numbers game: "If you want to close X deals, you need to get in front of Y prospects, etc." It's described this way because sales *is* a numbers game. While those with killer closing techniques do sell a higher percentage of the prospects they get in front of; they still need to get in front of prospects.

This makes sense. The more prospects they present, the more deals they close.

However, for unsuccessful sales teams, way too much attention is paid to the art of closing those in front of the salesperson and way too little to the art of getting the salesperson in front of more prospects.

If you're trying to create a team of winners, your primary focus should be on getting them in front of more prospects. Refining their closing skills is important, but not nearly as important as ensuring they're actively prospecting.

The math is simple, and it always works. If you have a salesperson who closes X% of the prospects she gets in front of, and you want to help her double her sales, she needs to get in front of twice as many prospects. Yes, you could teach her to close at 2X… in a perfect world… where the reason she was only closing X% was because she lacked the skills to close at a higher rate… and only if X% was an unacceptable rate.

Improving one's closing skills hits the law of diminishing returns rather quickly, while sales activities that put the salesperson in front of more prospects is only limited by time and efficiency. (For example: Do they have the time to make more phone calls, and are they maximizing the use of their time?)

Creating Self-Sustaining Winners

You're probably tired of my good news/great news of sales management, but I need to reiterate it here to underscore the need for your involvement in creating winners:

> The good news is that if salespeople always did what we wanted them to do, we never would've invented sales managers. The great news is this means you only need to train and reinforce best practices every single day for the rest of your working life.

But… there's even better than great news. When you consistently and constantly apply the principles of this book, you'll not only create winners, you'll begin to create self-sustaining winners. That is, you'll have salespeople who once required daily training and reinforcement, and now only need weekly… monthly… or "every now and then" training and reinforcement. They'll have become self-sustaining!

To create a team of self-sustaining winners requires just a tad more than the attitude and activity lessons already learned. While properly driving attitude and activity will definitely create winners today, the best way to ensure you're not spending all your time reinforcing these is to begin driving good habits in your sales team.

These habits are kind of the boring stuff that are essential for sales success.

Your attitude will become contagious… check. Activity completion and working on moneymakers will become the norm… great. These will drive increased employee satisfaction and higher paychecks, while reducing negative turnover… outstanding!

As you approach this point in your sales team's evolution, some of what you and they do can be put on autopilot. Keeping the team successful while on autopilot, however, requires they also focus on their most important moneymaker.

Their Most Important Moneymaker

If a concert violinist wants to be successful, they need to take extra special care of their violin. It is their only moneymaker – their most important asset – and a broken or out-of-tune moneymaker just won't do. Like a concert violinist, each of your salespeople needs to take extra special care of their most important asset: themselves.

If someone wants to truly be successful in sales – for the long term – they must ensure their most important instrument is always in great shape and ready to go. And while we've all known top sellers who can party all night, crawl out of bed after a couple of hours of sleep, down a few energy drinks, and hit the bricks; the truth is these sellers eventually burn out… or flame out.

What their bodies could handle in their twenties and thirties, they learn life is much different in their forties and fifties. Alcoholism, drug abuse, divorce, poor health, and other personal issues have derailed the professional careers of even the most promising salespeople.

Salespeople are their own fine-tuned Stradivarius; and if they don't take care of themselves; they will eventually stop working – just like a broken violin. Plus, you need their whole head in the game (so to speak), and when they're distracted by personal issues – or even if they just aren't getting enough sleep – you get less than you need.

As their manager, it's your duty to ensure both their short-term and long-term success. For the long term, this means you should help them develop healthy, great habits that will keep them productive long into the future.

If you genuinely care about your team, you'll want them to be successful today and tomorrow.

Healthy Habits

If you want your sellers to be successful this year, and in ten, twenty, and thirty years, you need to help them create healthy habits that can carry their bodies through the next few decades without breaking down. This means helping them add lots of boring habits and jettisoning those fun, cool habits they might have. For example:

- Encourage them to get enough sleep. Our bodies repair themselves when we sleep; and trying to do it all is just not possible over the long term if your sellers deprive their bodies – and especially their brains – of the sleep they need to function. Lack of sleep increases your sellers' risk of heart disease, diabetes, obesity, and depression. It also negatively impacts their brains' ability to remember (like how to overcome an objection) and its ability to comprehend (like recognizing buying signals).

- Help them to stop smoking or vaping. Salespeople who smoke not only stink when sitting across from a non-smoking prospect, but also become agitated more easily when a deal takes too long to complete. I've seen smokers and vapers blow deals with their customers because their mood changes as their need for a nicotine fix increases.

- Teach them to eat sensible meals. Any salesperson can go a few weeks eating nothing but fast food and seem to function properly; the problems arise when a salesperson never eats anything other than this crap. The long-term negative impacts of a poor diet are more than just the added pounds and the loss of energy they might notice after eating mostly fast food for a month or so. For those sellers who want to always remain at the top of their game, every ounce of energy counts. A great diet delivers this energy.

- Help them avoid energy drinks. Today's energy drinks are akin to the "pep pills" some salespeople routinely took to compensate for their lack of sleep in the last century. Yes, the initial boost of energy is great, but they cannot continue to ask their bodies to do more than designed by fooling it into thinking they've got energy to spare. If they need more than a couple of cups of coffee in the morning to get their bodies and brains going, they're likely in for an energy crash that could last for a very long time. Energy drinks are the liquid equivalent of fast food. That is, there appear to be few negative implications in the short term, though they can lead to all the same harmful health consequences when these become their staple beverage for months or years.

- Teach them to be happy. Yes, being happy is a habit a salesperson can develop. Therefore, encourage them to be happy for their coworkers, their company, and their customers. Their happiness will become contagious and others will be happy for them.

- Keep them away from negative chatter and thoughts. Sitting in the smoking circle complaining about the company's advertising or the HR Director might make them feel like they're bonding with others, but these negative thoughts will become like poison and sink an otherwise promising career.

- Encourage a healthy lifestyle. You can do this by staying healthy yourself, and by encouraging others to join you in healthy endeavors. For example, if you like to run, invite everyone on the team to join you for a 5K race in town. However, don't pressure anyone to become a clone of you. Not everyone is into the same off-work activities, and some of us absolutely hate running.

- Teach them the value of proper grooming. Customers will never complain when a salesperson is clean, fresh, and dressed nicely. This doesn't necessarily mean a suit and tie or a formal dress, but it does mean wearing clean clothes over a showered, clean body that smells good (use cologne or perfume sparingly).

- Don't celebrate or encourage alcohol consumption. You can and should enjoy your life; the same goes for your salespeople. However, be careful about the alcohol conversations that can dominate too many mornings in the sales world. No need to become a teetotaler, just refrain from making alcohol the centerpiece of your world or theirs, and certainly limit the alcohol at company functions.

Great habits might be boring, but they are essential for successfully selling over the long term. Moreover, great habits drive energy levels, and energy levels dictate everything from passion to mood. The bottom line is that passionate salespeople who are in a great mood outsell everyone else.

The great news is that your customers will feed off your salespeople's passion and energy. Buying anything should be an exciting time for your customers, and no one wants to buy from a smelly, disheveled, moody prick.

Oh, and these healthy habits aren't just meant for your sellers. Sales managers who live by these bring real (not manufactured) energy and passion to their jobs for the long term.

Strict Sales Processes Make a Difference

One final set of habits to consider involve your sales processes. While these can be a little awkward and painful when first introduced, they become smooth and easy when they become habits.

Top sellers don't freelance with every prospect. Quite the contrary – top sellers are known for treating prospects essentially the same and sticking to a strict sales process regardless of which rabbit hole a customer tries to take them down. They do this because they know process outsells everything else. It always has, and it always will.

By consistently and constantly reinforcing these, you'll begin creating habits in your sellers that eventually make them self-sustaining winners.

Tough Love

My apologies, but time for some negative coaching. That is, I'll be telling you what not to do – something I've tried to not lean on too much in this book because it's a lousy way to get a lesson across.

While you may have grown your sales career thanks to the tough love approach of your first sales manager, this approach does not work today. Tough love in the workplace, for the uninitiated, is basically a leadership style designed to make someone better by forcing them to take responsibility for their own actions and success.

You might think there's nothing wrong with that approach; after all, it's how you succeeded.

I'll argue that you *overcame* that tough love approach and succeeded anyway. You were self-motivated and had a desire to succeed. Moreover, you remained focused on what was important to you, and you sacrificed the fun (timewasters) for the profitable (moneymakers) all on your own.

Like all top sellers in tough love environments, you were rare. Your manager's approach had little impact on you; but it certainly had a negative impact on those salespeople who came and went. Tough love works in sales for those already driven to succeed. For everyone else, it ensures failure.

Plus, for today's crop of new salespeople, there are more timewasters available than there likely were in your day. Depending on your age, you may have started your sales career before smartphones, car phones, or even pagers. The equivalent of Tweets were quick quips posted above the urinals.

Employing a tough love approach today with a new salesperson is like buying a potted plant and denying it water. Tough love today is simply a refusal to help your team succeed. As one tough love manager told me recently, "They should know what to do! I'm not going to do it for them; and I'm not their damn babysitter!"

Correct, correct, and dead wrong. Correct, they should know what to do. Correct, you're not going to do it for them. Dead wrong if you think you're not their babysitter.

Just like a babysitter, as their manager, you're responsible for them from the time they clock in until the time they go home. You're responsible for their safety, and you're responsible for everything they do and don't do.

It's why, as we say, you get the big bucks.

You're Not a Football Coach

Tough love works in football.

Although we call them your sales *team*, successfully leading them is not even close to the same thing as successfully leading a sports team. While hard-nosed, my-way-or-the-highway football coaches like Bill Belichick and Nick Sabin drive success via their own brand of the no-nonsense, tough love approach, trying to run your sales team the same way Belichick runs the Patriots guarantees failure.

Being a member of the New England Patriots or Alabama Crimson Tide is a privilege; it's something some players dream about their entire lives. No offense, but being a member of your team is a job for most salespeople; it's something they never really saw themselves doing… but here they are.

Getting the most out of your team requires more than just showing them the door and telling them if they can't cut it, they shouldn't let the door hit them on the ass on the way out.

The Privilege is Yours

If your goal is to lead a team of winners, then the privilege must be yours. You should see leading them as a privilege, not the other way around. You should feel lucky they work for you, not the other way around.

Your job is to make each of your salespeople feel like the most important person in your life, not the other way around. This means dumping the tough love approach and becoming their advocate; doing everything in your power (short of doing their jobs for them) to help them succeed.

When the privilege is yours, you're poised to create winners; to build your own team of true superstars. A team that will arrive each day with a great attitude and ready for work. More importantly, a team that won't leave you when the unsuccessful sales manager across town runs a help wanted ad looking for true superstars.

…

KEY LEARNINGS:

- Successful sales managers create and maintain their own team of true superstars.

- They do this by constantly and consistently applying the principles detailed in this book.

- This creates habits, and great habits drive success in the long term, making their job and your job easier.

CHAPTER EXERCISES:

- Beginning today, and for at least the next week, you're going to make sure every salesperson (and every support person) knows what a privilege it is for you to have them on your team. This can be as simple as telling them this directly – though be sure you mean it – or as involved as catering in a team lunch/dinner every day for a week as you declare this week "My Privilege Week" or even a funny and sappy "You Complete Me Week."

- A longer-term exercise from this chapter involves instilling the personal habits we introduced. This doesn't mean crossing the HR line or having interventions with your salespeople, though it does mean modeling and discussing the kinds of habits you want your team to adopt. Begin to celebrate the boring things like a good night's sleep, exercise, punctuality, sobriety, a healthy diet, etc.

22

THE LEGACY SELLERS

Here's the situation: You took over an existing team that includes a few "top" sales guys or gals, and it was explained to you that some or all of these "top" sellers might be a little quirky… so, just let them do what they do and stay out of their way.

Of course, after a few days you discover these "top" sellers are prima donnas hitting mediocre numbers while doing very little actual work. They're either living off a small percentage of their prior customers returning or they're burning through your fresh prospects (or both).

They've stuck around because their sales volume is enough to cover their nut, and because the managers leave them alone. In fact, you might have even been warned that these "top" guys and gals might quit if you push them too hard.

Oh. The. Humanity.

The primary route unsuccessful sales managers take with legacy sellers is to just leave them alone. Let them sell their few deals and stay out of their way. They'll convince themselves this is what's best for the team, as it allows the manager to focus on those who want to learn and improve.

But it never quite works out that way.

Stop Rewarding Legacy Sellers

Yes, over the last two chapters I've told you to be satisfied and to create winners from your existing team… and I still mean exactly that, especially with legacy sellers.

In automotive retail, we sometimes give these guys and gals a nickname based on the number of units they average and their first name. Even if they don't call them this, virtually every dealership has an 8-Car Alan (perhaps yours is a 10-Car Ted or even a 14-Car Phoebe). They are the veteran salespeople who deliver an unspectacular, yet steady volume of units each month. They've been with the dealership for more than a dozen years and the (unsuccessful) managers appreciate their loyalty.

The problem is loyalty should be a two-way street. The company is loyal to them, but they're not loyal to the company. Yes, their butt has been in the same seat for years, but that's not loyalty. In fact, you know they're not loyal because you've been told not to push them too hard for fear they'll quit.

They believe the list of past customers are *their* customers, not the company's. They give the company no credit for the millions spent marketing and maintaining the dealership during their tenure. They're convinced their success is theirs and theirs alone, and they don't like being told what to do… especially from some new manager.

Don't you dare try to tell them to call their past customers!

They know their customers, not you; and they'll decide when it's right to call them… which turns out to be never. But, let one of their prior customers buy without asking for them and they'll be at your desk demanding credit for the sale.

If you've already employed the practices outlined in the second chapter ("The New Sales Manager"), then you've set the expectations for what comes next. (Of course, by the time you're reading this chapter, you've likely already solved the issues with any legacy sellers – that is, if you've been utilizing the lessons so far.)

The Math on Legacy Sellers

Many unsuccessful sales managers don't see the harm in just leaving the prima donnas alone. This is a big mistake, as these veterans poison and/or drive away your potential superstars.

New salespeople learn nothing from this group… except how to avoid moneymakers. Everyone sees the special treatment the legacy sellers receive, and they know it's not fair. Great (and *potentially* great) salespeople leave, while below average sellers hang around hoping to someday join this country club of do-nothings.

Oh, and legacy sellers cost you sales. To prove this, we'll do some quick back-of-the-napkin math. (We'll use 14-Car Phoebe and assume she's been selling vehicles for your dealership for 18 years.)

Eighteen years at 14 units per month means Phoebe has sold 3,024 vehicles. Not bad; but she's already been rewarded for these sales when you paid her the commissions, bonuses, spiffs, and other compensation over that time.

To stay on the conservative side and to make the math easy, let's assume half of the vehicles Phoebe sold over the last 18 years were to previous customers. This means she's sold to 1,512 different customers during her tenure.

Assuming the average consumer trades every six years, Phoebe has 252 customers who will replace their current vehicle this year. (She has 1,512 former customers, and one-sixth of them will buy each year. 1,512 divided by 6 equals 252.)

That's 21 per month, but Phoebe is only going to sell 14… and some of those (perhaps half or more) will be the fresh prospects she sells. Phoebe, you see, is only selling 7 units each month to a potential 21 allegedly "loyal" customers.

Are These Customers Truly Loyal to Phoebe?

Given the average household in America owns two cars, not one, Phoebe should be pulling in another 21 units for you each month – if her customers are truly loyal to her, right?

What about the referrals Phoebe should be receiving from her 1,512 previous customers? Great salespeople can generate up to two referrals from each sale. However, even if we only expect Phoebe to generate one referral per sale, that's another 21 potential units this month.

While some of the 1,512 previous customers moved out of the area or are deceased, the number of children these 1,512 previous customers have (that are now of driving age) balance out those no longer living in your market.

My math tells me she should be generating 63 units per month without selling any fresh prospects, yet she's only selling 14 (and only 7 of those to previous customers). Your 14-Car Phoebe is costing you more than 50 units each month… all because she refuses to follow processes and work her moneymakers.

It's Time for a Change

While I do not advocate firing your 14-Car Phoebe, it's clearly time for a change; a change, by the way, that must start at the top and be enforced every day by all managers. You're rewarding Phoebe's laziness by making sure she gets the first crack if one of her prior customers happens to walk into the dealership.

To be clear, whenever a prior customer walks in on their own, you got lucky. There are too many choices out there to assume those who bought from you before will buy from you again once they catch New Car Fever. They're going to go online and be bombarded with choices, prices, terms, trade values, and everything else they need to make an informed decision before they ever set foot on any lot... even yours.

The change is simple. Create a few rules and enforce them.

The key, of course, is enforcement; sometimes called accountability. Accountability does not mean punishment, it means accountability. For every sales manager reading this, you're already held accountable by your salespeople; even by lazy salespeople like 14-Car Phoebe.

Phoebe expects to be paid for the 14 units she sold this month; so, that's what you do. For eighteen years, Phoebe has held your company accountable for the commissions, bonuses, spiffs, and other compensation you and your predecessors told her she could earn by selling cars. You've held up your end of the bargain; it's time for Phoebe to hold up hers.

Rewarding the Right Salespeople

Sales managers should want to reward aggressive salespeople. Those willing to help every fresh prospect, make their assigned phone calls, work their moneymakers, and diligently (and properly) use their CRM. Well... then... let's do that.

Every industry is a little different, so I'm going to stick with automotive retail and our Phoebe example to illustrate how writing and enforcing a few simple rules will increase Phoebe's production and the overall sales for her dealership.

For automotive sales teams, there are just a few simple rules you need to put in place and enforce to change your rewards system from one that benefits those unwilling to follow processes to those hungry for a chance to sell 20, 30, or even 50 units a month.

Good business rules – those that are simple, fair, designed to improve performance, and are consistently enforced – are welcomed by top sellers and those who want to become top sellers.

The simplest rule is called the Protected Prospects Rule. With this rule, we're going to "protect" Phoebe's prospects for her provided she follows just a few simple guidelines. For example, Phoebe will be protected and will receive full credit for any sales made under any of the following situations:

- Her prospect arrived for an appointment, on time, set by Phoebe.

- Her prospect arrived without an appointment, though asked for her by name within earshot of a manager or the receptionist… on a day Phoebe is working.

- Her prospect was in the store earlier today, and Phoebe properly documented the visit in the CRM before they returned.

However, Phoebe is not protected and gets no credit for the sale if any of the following occur:

- A prospect arrives on Phoebe's day off and buys from another salesperson.

- A prospect arrives without an appointment, doesn't ask for Phoebe within earshot of a manager or the receptionist, and is assisted and sold by someone else.

Unsuccessful sales managers (and Phoebe) would argue that Phoebe deserves some credit for repeat buyers who arrive on her day off or don't ask for her. This is why they're unsuccessful sales managers and why Phoebe only sells 14 each month when she should be selling 60+.

Let's be clear; if one of Phoebe's prior customers arrives on her day off – even if they ask for her – she deserves no credit for the sale. She deserves no credit because the dealership got lucky that (A) The customer chose to return to your store instead of shopping online and finding a better deal somewhere else, and (B) They weren't blown out by the salesperson who helped them.

Phoebe will argue the rule is not fair. Not fair? Not fair to whom? Not fair to Phoebe or not fair to the company? This rule is incredibly fair, as it rewards Phoebe for her sales activities (calling her former customers, setting appointments, etc.) while ensuring the company's database of prior customers is not neglected.

Of course, most of the 8-Car Alans, 10-Car Teds, and 14-Car Phoebes out there don't really have that many "loyal" customers. In fact, some of these customers don't even want to work with Phoebe again, though they are loyal to your dealership and/or brand.

The Protected Prospects Rule ensures that those who *do* want to work with Phoebe again may do so – provided she's working on the day they arrive. However, it also ensures that those who do not (and those who don't even remember her) get to work with the salesperson who greeted them.

Oh, and Phoebe? Well, perhaps she'll start making her calls and setting real appointments that show, instead of hoping her prior customers show up and buy.

Rules Matter

As I wrote earlier, process sells. Process, however, requires rules. Rules require consequences. Consequences mean accountability. Though accountability doesn't mean punishment. It means accountability… always. In bad times and good.

Good salespeople need structure and great salespeople want to know what's expected of them.

Can we all agree that your salespeople should be making calls? Can we all agree that they should be making calls every day? Can we all agree that these calls should include owner marketing calls to their current sold database?

Then why are unsuccessful sales managers rewarding lazy sellers for sitting on their collective rumps?'

When your prior customers decide on their own it's time to buy again, there is absolutely no guarantee they'll choose your company this time around. In fact, if you're in automotive retail, there's at least a 50% chance they won't even choose your brand this time.

In automotive retail, when you fail to set a firm appointment that shows, you're lucky to sell a car.

Every CRM database is gold; but like gold, it needs to be mined properly. This means, unless your team is busy calling their previously sold customers, there is no guarantee that these folks will buy from you (or even consider you) when they come back into the market.

For automotive retail, the average buyer today physically visits fewer than two dealerships before they buy. Guaranteeing the only chance you have to maximize your sales to prior customers is by proactively marketing to them in advance of their next car shopping excursion.

This means phone calls. This means birthday cards. This means greeting them when they service with you. This means using the CRM as it was intended – to manage your customer relations.

No Appointment; No Protection

The Protected Prospects Rule basically means "no appointment; no protection," and the only salespeople who don't want this rule in place are the ones unwilling to follow your processes and work their moneymakers – especially their customer database.

If someone on your team doesn't like this rule, it's because they're not making their required calls or using your approved talk tracks. Oh, and they don't like to be held accountable. Of course, the lack of accountability to required activities is most often the primary reason unsuccessful sales managers find themselves managing a team of mediocre sellers; and why they're blowing out every new seller they hire.

The great news for you is that rules like this one (when enforced) are Accountability 101 (without the need for much oversight). They either set the appointment or they lose the sale; and you no longer have to listen to endless he-said/she-said arguments from a team too lazy to call their own customers.

For all new rules, give your team a 30-day notice before putting them in place. For the Protected Prospects Rule, this will give them a month to call their current customers and begin setting appointments.

Certainly, the legacy sellers will see this rule as you taking *their* customers away and giving them to another salesperson. However, by not employing this rule, your legacy sellers are actually sending *your* customers to buy from your competition.

...

KEY LEARNINGS:

- Legacy sellers are not inherently bad, they just need your guidance and direction… and some accountability.

- If you're worried about someone quitting over being asked to do their job, you probably need to rethink your own career choices.

- Rules matter; and when your rules are fair and designed to drive better results, every salesperson will sell more.

CHAPTER EXERCISES:

- Write down 3-5 behaviors you want from all salespeople (making calls, working a database, etc.) that will lead to better results.

- Write at least one rule that will drive those behaviors and ask someone you trust to review it. Is it fair? Does it make sense? Will you enforce it?

- Present this rule to your team with at least a 30-day notice.

23

SPINNING THE PLATES

Some readers may remember when Johnny Carson hosted *The Tonight Show*, or when Mike Douglas and Dick Cavett ran daytime talk shows. In those days, talk shows would often have magicians and circus-type acts perform live for the audience.

While today's talk shows might, on rare occasion, host a magician or part of the cast from a Cirque du Soleil show, they've grown too sophisticated to showcase the one made-for-TV circus act that enthralled me in my youth: the plate spinner.

Plate spinners basically spun plates or other dishes on long sticks. They'd start at one end of the stage, get the first plate spinning on a stick, then move down the line until all the plates were spinning at once. The trick was to keep the plates spinning; and this required the plate spinner to constantly move among the sticks, expertly shaking them to speed up each individual spinning plate. Just as the spinner recovered one nearly dropped plate, he or she would quickly move to recover another.

Successful sales management is a lot like spinning plates. Just as you reenergize, refocus, or resolve one seller, process, or situation, you'll find you need to move quickly to handle another.

Maintaining High Performance

Virtually every change you inspire in each individual seller will need to be maintained and reinforced over time. That's where the plate spinning comes into play. Let me give you a quick example that might help all readers understand what I mean.

Let's say we could accurately grade salespeople's attitudes on a scale of 1-10. Of course, you're working to get everyone to a 10. However, even when you feel you've helped a seller improve their attitude about sales, the customers, the company, etc. enough to reach that level, your work is not done... it's never done.

To be a successful sales manager, you must monitor and maintain everything that makes each individual seller successful. In the case of the salesperson with the "10" attitude, be prepared to check in with them on a daily or near-daily basis to keep this plate spinning. Just because someone is a 10 today doesn't mean they're going to be a 10 tomorrow.

As your team improves, you'll find you need to spend less and less time keeping the plates spinning for your sellers. In fact, with the right leadership, some salespeople will maintain their high-performance levels as if on autopilot.

Maintenance Mode

Most successful sales managers eventually find they're in maintenance mode. That is, they're not spending much time recruiting and hiring, they're not panicking at the end of each month trying to reach some goal they ignored for the last three weeks, and they're not constantly correcting bad behavior.

They're still spinning plates, but each time they shake the stick to propel a plate faster, it's easier than the last time they had to do this… the plates spin longer… some seem to never stop spinning.

Maintenance mode isn't a vacation, of course; your team still needs you to train and reinforce best practices every single day for the rest of your working life. However, you will find you're required to spend less time doing those activities; leaving you more time to explore ways to grow even more.

You can test new processes and methods.

You can demo a new shiny object some vendor swore would double your sales.

You can search for great future sales candidates (assuming your sales growth will require additional salespeople).

You can spend extra time developing someone on your team to eventually replace you (or to just cover for you when you take your next well-deserved vacation).

You can give more attention to your company's marketing and lead-acquisition activities.

You can do whatever you want that will drive the business forward.

Marketing is Not Sales

Oh, and because I mentioned marketing, I need to ensure we're all on the same page with this. Marketing is not sales.

I don't care what's written on your business cards. Sales is not marketing, and marketing is not sales. Additionally, despite the title of some company vice president, and no matter how often these are said in the same sentence, sales and marketing are not the same thing.

I tell you this because too many sales managers depend on their company's marketing to drive a good week, month, or year. Marketing is important; however, waiting for or relying on marketing/advertising to drive your growth is a fool's errand.

Successful sales managers control their success.

Even if your job duties include overseeing marketing and advertising, or you're in maintenance mode and want to dip your toe into the company's advertising pool, it's important to look at the sales and marketing functions as two separate silos. Again, marketing is important… but, it ain't sales.

Manage the Activities, Not the Results

If unsuccessful managers actually manage anything, they manage the results. That is, they look at the numbers each salesperson put up at the end of the month and then tell everyone whether they did a good job or a bad job.

While results are certainly important, there is a fallacy to results management. When you manage only the results (and not how the salespeople attained the results), your team will begin to shortcut your processes. This makes generating results tomorrow, next week, and next month that much harder.

Eventually, managers tracking only the results have no idea how to achieve greater volumes because they aren't managing the inputs that drive the results. In other words, they're not managing the activities. They won't know why sales are up or down, or even which salespeople are doing their jobs well and which ones are just getting lucky. They won't be able to distinguish a 15-car seller who works her database and earns every sale she makes from a 15-car seller who burns through their opportunities (and yours), destroying long-term relationships, and seeing twice as many prospects as the average seller in the store.

Managing the activities keeps you constantly focused on what's important. Managing the activities is not micro-management, it's keeping your team productive and efficient by driving the activities. As I wrote in an earlier chapter, driving activities is the best thing a sales manager can do for his or her team.

Oh, and when you manage the activities, the results will come.

It's Not the Technology

While a great CRM and other tech tools will help a successful sales manager keep the plates spinning, it's not the technology that really matters, it's the technician. This is precisely why unsuccessful sales managers do not suddenly become successful when the company adds a new technology tool to their arsenal.

If you're willing to rely solely on technology to lead your team, it begs the question: Why do we need you? Over the long term, technology costs less than a sales manager, is never late or sick, and we don't have to pay any benefits.

The best CRM with great follow-up processes and the finest and most accurate tracking tools don't matter if you're not willing to lead. Additionally, I've never met a salesperson who couldn't fake out the best CRM and tracking tools. So, if you're not elbows deep inspecting the activities, be prepared for reports that show everyone worked hard all month, yet still missed their goals.

Good Stress / Bad Stress

Imagine if you were literally spinning plates on national television. The cameras, the lights, the studio audience… yikes. That would be too stressful for most people to handle.

Unsuccessful sales managers feel stress. Successful sales managers feel stress. The difference is the type of stress each feels. Stress, you see, is not always a bad thing. Stress is simply our brain's response to changes or demands in daily life.

There are two types of stress our brains can create, and our bodies can feel. These are called distress and eustress. And without getting too deep into the medical field, distress is bad, eustress is good.

Eustress helps to motivate us. It allows us to focus our energies on what's important, and it improves performance. Eustress exists within the realm of things we can control.

Conversely, distress is demotivational. It causes anxiety and it reduces our ability to perform at our best. Moreover, distress often leads to mental and/or physical issues. Distress most often exists outside the realm of things we can control.

Stress in a Bad Month

Even successful sales managers can find their teams in a mid-month hole. The difference for them, as it relates to stress, is that because they're in control, driving activities, and modeling a great attitude, the stress they most often feel in these situations is eustress. They know the levers to pull to ensure they close out the month strong; and they know which levers are just short-term fixes that will leave them in a hole next month, so they avoid these.

For unsuccessful managers finding their teams in a mid-month hole (again), the stress they feel is almost always distress. It's demotivating; and the bad feelings distress creates in the manager are projected onto the salespeople. Now everyone is in some state of distress… and it's unproductive.

Everyone on the team feels distress because of one or more of these common causes of negative stress on the job:

- My boss or company is asking for too much (excessive demands).

- They want perfection (unrealistic expectations).

- I might get fired (lack of job security).

- I don't know what to do (lack of proper training).

- My boss/coworker is a jerk (team conflicts).

- I don't have the power to… (no authority to make necessary decisions).

- Things keep changing (lack of control / no foresight).

- I've got too much to do today (overscheduling).

- I'm way behind (procrastination / activity avoidance).

Your commitment to attitude and activity, and your willingness to keep the plates spinning reduce distress and drive eustress. Moreover, when you see your plate-spinning duties as productive, you welcome the eustress this creates.

…

KEY LEARNINGS:

- Maintaining high performance is not a one-and-done or set-it-and-forget-it activity. Maintaining high performance requires sales managers to become adept at keeping all the plates spinning.

- Manage the activities, and the results will come.

- Stress is not necessarily bad. Successful sales managers (and their teams) thrive on eustress, as they encounter very little distress in their work lives.

CHAPTER EXERCISES:

- Review the nine bullet points listed under "Stress in a Bad Month" and identify those your individual salespeople could be experiencing.

- Create a plan to eliminate these. Some (like "I don't know what to do") require you to create a detailed blueprint for each seller to resolve. Others (like "I might get fired") require nothing more than for you to spend more time with each seller and provide positive coaching on a daily or near-daily basis.

24

THE "SECRETS"

While most leadership guides start with a list of traits, I intentionally saved the "secrets" to successful sales management for the end of this book. My rationale is that those managers who most need to change their behavior, style, or approach (the unsuccessful sales managers) will see a list of traits and simply post them in the workplace.

This gives them a feeling of accomplishment. Moreover, they believe by posting these traits they're proving to the world these traits describe them. This isn't a checklist; these aren't hollow sayings on posters you hang in the breakroom; these are traits that you internalize and live every day.

The Dirty Dozen – 12 "Secrets" of Successful Sales Managers

They're Authentic. Successful sales managers are honest and authentic. They show their true self – warts and all – to their teams. Their salespeople appreciate this and, as a result, are more likely to trust their sales managers at every turn.

They're Optimistic. Simply put, optimists see challenges as opportunities; pessimists see them as overwhelming obstacles. Optimistic sales managers know their work will pay off; pessimistic ones think "Why even try?"

They're Fair. Because they're fair, their teams are willing to do more and try more. Unfair sales managers instill fear in their teams – even in their top performers – because no one knows the consequences of any good or bad actions. When you're seen as fair, your team trusts you, and when employees trust their boss, they're less likely to leave, take sick days, or shirk important responsibilities.

They're Learners. Successful sales managers know they don't have all the answers, so they're always open to new ideas from everyone and from everywhere.

They're Curious. Being open to new ideas is important, but successful sales managers are also curious. This means they're actively seeking new ideas to improve their own team's results.

They're Decisive. Successful sales managers know that making no decision is worse than making a bad decision. So, while they'd prefer to always make good decisions, they're willing to risk a bad decision made for good reasons. Indecision can quickly destroy an otherwise productive sales team; and top sellers don't want to work for those suffering from analysis paralysis.

They're Focused. Because they know each day can be different, successful sales managers never allow today's distractions to remove their focus on those activities that can drive the greatest results in both the short and long term.

They're Dissatisfied. You may not always see it, but successful sales managers believe in the power of continuous process improvement. This means that even after a record month, they're quick to look for better, more efficient, and/or more effective ways, methods, and/or marketing to drive even stronger results next time.

They're Fearless. Being fearless allows successful sales managers to be open to new ideas, try new methods, take risks, and heap the praise for their success on others.

They're Thinkers. They know every action has consequences, so they're thoughtful in how and when they make changes or how they introduce anything new to their team. This doesn't mean they're afraid to share with their team or that they would lie to keep their team motivated. To the contrary, they just know nothing happens in a vacuum, so they consider the outcomes of their actions before acting.

They're Principled. Driven to always do what's right, successful sales managers are guided by their unwavering principles. This sometimes brings them the respect of their peers, and more importantly, always earns them the respect of their team.

They're Servants. Above all else, successful sales managers "work" for their salespeople, not the other way around. They are often more committed to a seller's individual success than the sellers are themselves.

What About Talent?

Some of you may have noticed what's not included in this list: Talent. Talent is overrated in sales management. When it comes to talent in salespeople, it's often just an excuse used by weak sales managers to explain the difference between the salesperson on the top and those near the bottom. You see, by blaming someone's lack of sales success on a lack of talent, a sales manager doesn't have to take responsibility for that salesperson's failure.

Neither leadership nor sales is some sport where God-given abilities (aka talent) can make the difference between two otherwise well-meaning, hardworking individuals. Talent is meaningless when it comes to sales success; as hard work beats talent on any day ending in a "Y."

Oh, Just One More Thing…

Successful sales managers… strike that. Successful leaders use fewer words and hold fewer meetings than their less successful peers. Successfully leading a sales team is not about telling, it's about doing. Doing all the things you learned in this book.

Instead of rambling speeches, rants, and long meetings, successful leaders use MBWA and real-time coaching to drive the activities that ensure success for everyone on the team.

Sales is not hard; it just takes work.

Successful sales management is also not hard; it too just takes work.

Good selling!

…

KEY LEARNINGS:

- Posting the twelve traits of successful sales managers will not make you successful; but it could be a start.

- Talent is overrated.

- When you consider these twelve in total, the word humility should come to mind. Ego is important to individual success, though humility is required for team success.

CHAPTER EXERCISES:

- Because we all have a distorted view of our own strengths and weaknesses, this exercise must involve others. Though be careful, you might not like what you hear. Of course, if you're a terrible leader, you're probably going to hear nothing but glowing praise when completing this exercise. Walk through the list of twelve "secrets" (and the explanations) with each of your sellers. Ask them to evaluate you on a scale of 1-10 on these, one by one. Where you score below an eight on any trait, ask them to give you either an example of why they think that way or what they think you could do to earn a ten.